Wiley Keys to Success

HOW TO STUDY
FOR SUCCESS

Beverly Ann Chin is Professor of English, Director of the English Teaching Program, former Director of the Montana Writing Project, and a former President of the National Council of Teachers of English.

Dr. Chin is a nationally recognized leader in English language arts standards curriculum, instruction, and assessment. Many schools and states call upon her to help them develop programs in reading and writing across the curriculum. Dr. Chin has edited and written numerous books and articles in the field of English language arts. She is the author of *On Your Own: Writing* and *On Your Own: Grammar*.

Wiley Keys to Success

HOW TO STUDY FOR SUCCESS

Beverly Ann Chin, Ph.D.

Series Consultant

WILEY

John Wiley & Sons, Inc.

Developed, Designed and Produced by BOOK BUILDERS LLC

Published by John Wiley & Sons, Inc., Hoboken, New Jersey
Published simultaneously in Canada

For general information about our other products and services, please contact our Customer Care Department within the United States at (800) 762-2974, outside the United States at (317) 572-3993 or fax (317) 572-4002.

Wiley also publishes its books in a variety of electronic formats. Some content that appears in print may not be available in electronic books. For more information about Wiley products, visit our web site at www.wiley.com.

Library of Congress Cataloging-in-Publication Data:

How to study for success / Beverly Ann Chin, series consultant.
    p. cm.
  Includes index.
  ISBN 0-471-43155-9 (pbk. : alk. paper)
1. Study skills—Juvenile literature. I. Chin, Beverly Ann.
LB1601.H69 2004
371.3'028'1—dc22

                                                    2004002225

Printed in the United States of America

10 9 8 7 6 5 4 3 2 1

DEAR STUDENTS

Welcome to the **WILEY KEYS TO SUCCESS** series! The books in this series are practical guides designed to help you be a better student. Each book focuses on an important area of schoolwork, including building your vocabulary, studying and doing homework, writing research papers, taking tests, and more.

Each book contains seven chapters—the keys to helping you improve your skills as a student. As you understand and use each key, you'll find that you will enjoy learning more than ever before. As a result, you'll feel more confident in your classes and be better prepared to demonstrate your knowledge.

I invite you to use the **WILEY KEYS TO SUCCESS** series at school and at home. As you apply each key, you will open the doors to success in school as well as to success in many other areas of your life. Good luck, and enjoy the journey!

Beverly Ann Chin, Series Consultant

Professor of English

University of Montana, Missoula

Note to Teachers, Librarians, and Parents

The **WILEY KEYS TO SUCCESS** series is a series of handbooks designed to help students improve their academic performance. Happily, the keys can open doors for everyone—at home, in school, at work.

Each book is an invaluable resource that offers seven simple, practical steps to mastering an important aspect of schoolwork, such as building vocabulary, studying and doing homework, taking tests, and writing research papers. We hand readers seven keys—or chapters—that show them how to increase their success as learners—a plan intended to build lifelong learning skills. Reader-friendly graphics, self-assessment questions, and comprehensive appendices provide additional information.

Helpful features scattered throughout the books include "Learning It Right," which expands on the text with charts, graphs, and models; "Inside Secret," which reveals all-important hints, rules, definitions, and even warnings; and "Ready, Set, Review," which makes it easy for students to remember key points.

WILEY KEYS TO SUCCESS *series is designed to ensure that all students have the opportunity to experience success.* Once students know achievement, they are more likely to become independent learners, effective communicators, and critical thinkers. Many readers will want to use each guidebook by beginning with the first key and progressing systematically to the last key. Some readers will select the keys they need most and integrate what they learn with their own routines.

As educators and parents, you can encourage students to use the books in this series to assess their own strengths and weaknesses as learners. Using students' responses and your own observations of their study skills and habits, you can help students develop positive attitudes, set realistic goals, form successful schedules, organize materials, and monitor their own academic progress. In addition, you can discuss how adults use similar study strategies and communication skills in their personal and professional lives.

We hope you and your students will enjoy the **WILEY KEYS TO SUCCESS** series. We think readers will turn to these resources time and time again. By showing students how to achieve everyday success, we help children grow into responsible, independent young adults who value their education—and into adults who value learning throughout their lives.

Beverly Ann Chin, Series Consultant
Professor of English
University of Montana, Missoula

 CONTENTS

INTRODUCTION

Learning Styles: What They Are and

Why They're Important

Warning: This book is good for you. Uh-oh. We know what it means when something is called "good for you." Either it tastes bad, or it's boring. But don't put the book down yet. Sure, the most important feature of this book is that it can help you to be a better student. But other points about this book make it worth reading.

For one thing, it's easy to read. It was written for you to enjoy, as well as to learn how to use your study time more effectively. This book was written with the goal of being informative but not dull. Sometimes it's even funny. There are cartoons and other illustrations along the way.

This book deals with every aspect of studying. It explains how to prepare, how to take full advantage of class time, and how to make the most of homework and assignments. It even covers little details that can make a big difference—like eating the right foods before studying, choosing the right classroom seat, and overcoming shyness in class (if that's a problem).

One section of this book gives valuable tips on how to take advantage of a computer—and how to avoid computer disasters, too. These days, knowing about computers has become more important than ever.

Finally, as you'll find out in a few pages, this book has valuable lessons for *everyone*, regardless of how you're doing in school and what you expect your future to hold.

KEY 1

GET READY TO STUDY NOW

✓ **Wanting to Learn**

✓ **Having the Right Supplies**

✓ **Setting Up a Good Work Space**

Let's face it. Many students do not like to study much. You will see here why studying matters.

Many students come up with lots of excuses to avoid or put off studying. You probably know some of those excuses. Maybe you even use them yourself now and then. They include lines like: "I'm not a good student whether I study or not." " I don't plan to go to college, so studying is a waste of my time." "I'll never get science (or math or history), so why bother?" "My memory's so good that I don't need to study." And so on.

What you need to know, first of all, is that all of these excuses—and any others that people think up—have one important thing in common—they're wrong! Want to know why? Just keep reading. You will see why studying matters and how it can really make a difference for you when you do it right.

Wanting to Learn

Everyone needs to study, including you. The sooner you develop good and effective study habits, the more automatic and easy they become for you. The best time to get to work on it is *now*.

Good study skills are important, whether you're the kind of student who learns quickly or one who takes a little longer to master all the information. Whichever category you fit into, you can achieve more in school with better study habits. True, those students who try hardest will benefit most, but even those who usually get high grades find worthwhile results from a more effective study routine. Keep in mind that as you advance to higher grades, the work gets more demanding. The good habits you develop now become even more valuable later on.

Whatever you do in adult life requires you to study something. To get a driver's license, you must take and pass a written test based on information you study in a manual. Even after you finish school, you are not done with studying. Almost any job requires you to put in study time. For example, if you become an automobile mechanic, you must study to keep up with developments in engine design so you can maintain the newer cars. To work in the postal service, law enforcement, or any government-connected job, you must pass exams.

Here is another important reason for studying well. Success and self-confidence go together. Nothing builds self-confidence like success, in school and elsewhere. You can make the best possible start toward success and self-confidence by working on your study habits.

In addition to these long-term reasons to study, you can make up short-range ones to keep you going. Every now and then, you can give yourself little rewards for spending periods of time on work that you don't enjoy for its own sake. Do you like to listen to music? Do you have favorite TV shows or sports events that you enjoy watching? Maybe you love nothing better than hanging out with a group of friends at someone's house or the mall. Try putting in some serious study time on that challenging course work, and then reward yourself by doing one of your favorite things.

You may want to make a chart like the one which lists long-range and short-range motivations. Keep it handy, and look it over now and then. It can help you to focus on what you need to do and why you need to do it.

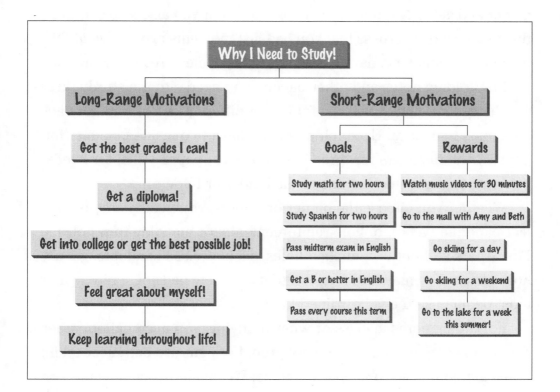

Why I Need to Study!

Long-Range Motivations

- Get the best grades I can!
- Get a diploma!
- Get into college or get the best possible job!
- Feel great about myself!
- Keep learning throughout life!

Short-Range Motivations

Goals
- Study math for two hours
- Study Spanish for two hours
- Pass midterm exam in English
- Get a B or better in English
- Pass every course this term

Rewards
- Watch music videos for 30 minutes
- Go to the mall with Amy and Beth
- Go skiing for a day
- Go skiing for a weekend
- Go to the lake for a week this summer!

Consider giving yourself bigger rewards for bigger achievements. For instance, if you get a good final grade on a tough course, treat yourself to a day at the beach or to tickets to that big concert. Just remember to be honest about whether or not you met the goal you set before giving yourself a reward. And don't get so distracted by thinking about the reward that it interferes with doing the work!

Having the Right Supplies

Imagine that you are ready to start baking a cake or fixing your bicycle. You're eager to start—until you suddenly realize that you don't have all the ingredients or the right tools that you need to do the work! How irritating—and time-consuming—that becomes! You have to stop working to find what is missing, or, worse, you may need to go out and get it. Not only do you lose time, but you also lose some of the energy and eagerness that you had just moments ago. To avoid this when you're studying, have all the supplies you need ready and available.

For holding notes and other papers, you need either a sturdy three-ring loose-leaf binder or some folders of different colors, one for each class plus two extra. Each folder should have two inside pockets (for papers) and fasteners for three-hole loose-leaf paper. (Chapter 2 tells you how to make the best use of the binder or folders.)

Whether you choose the binder or folders, you need plenty of loose-leaf paper and a box of hole reinforcements for mending torn holes. For papers without prepunched holes, such as class handouts, get a hole punch. You may find it useful to have a few pads of scratch paper; most people use the yellow lined kind.

For taking notes in class or when studying, you need ballpoint pens. Yes, you need pencils (and erasers), too, but pens are better for taking notes that you need to keep for a while. Writing in pencil may fade or smear. It is no fun to look at notes taken, say, two months earlier, and find only a smudgy, unreadable mess. Pencils and pens that write in different colors are useful for note taking, as well as other purposes. (In Chapter 3, you'll learn more about taking notes.)

In addition, you need brightly colored markers in various colors— the felt-tipped kind. Standard felt-tipped markers are great for emphasizing especially important material to review. There's nothing like a bright red star in the margin of a page of notes to get your attention. *Highlighters* are felt-tipped pens specially designed for marking printed text. You can use them to color directly over notes or printed pages without hiding the writing underneath. Of course, you should *never* use highlighters or any kind of pen to mark up textbooks or other books that you do not own, like those from the library.

Other useful supplies include transparent adhesive tape, glue, rubber cement, paste, paper clips, and a stapler (plus extra staples). A ruler often comes in handy as well. In order to ensure that anything you lose or misplace gets back to you, use adhesive labels to label your supplies properly. This means that your labels should include your name, the name of your school, and maybe your teacher's name or your grade level—all legibly written.

Protect Your Textbooks

You should use book covers to protect your textbooks, either preprinted covers made for that purpose or ones you make yourself from sturdy wrapping paper. Make sure your book covers include your name and that of your school. Write that information legibly on the covers *before* putting them on the books to avoid marking the textbooks. You can use transparent tape to hold the covers in place, but avoid sticking tape to the books themselves, because when you peel the tape off, you are likely to peel pieces of the book away, too.

This list of supplies may not be complete, but it contains most of the things that you should have on hand. Depending on what you're studying,

LEARNING IT RIGHT

Model Supply List

When you have all your supplies, you'll feel eager to get to work. The next question is: "Where do I actually work?" To find out, keep reading.

School Supplies

three-ring binder	highlighters
loose-leaf paper	transparent adhesive tape
hole reinforcers	glue
hole punch	rubber cement
pads of scratch paper	paste
ballpoint pens	paper clips
#2 pencils with erasers	stapler and staples
colored pencils	ruler
colored felt-tipped markers	adhesive labels

KEY
1

your teacher may add items, possibly for specific classes or projects. For mathematics, you might need a compass, a protractor, graph paper, and a calculator (with extra batteries). For science or art projects, you may need an old shirt or an apron. For English language arts, you may need a dictionary, thesaurus, or style manual. Teachers may also have their own ideas on how you should label assignments, or they may have a preference about whether to use a loose-leaf binder or folders. Of course, you can make adjustments to your supplies based on what your teacher requires. The model supply list on page 6 can help you in gathering supplies. If you rewrite it to create your own list, leave some space at the end for any additional items your teacher may suggest.

Setting Up a Good Work Space

Having the right space to work in is as important as having the right attitude and the right supplies. A great work space helps you in different ways. It can save you time and allow you to make the most of each study session. A well-organized work space also helps you to save energy. And because it is a pleasant place to work, it helps you concentrate better.

Using the same familiar space for doing most of your work outside class is a good idea. If you have your own room at home, that is probably a good place for your work space. But if need be, you can find a good space elsewhere.

Your work space does not have to be huge, but it should be big enough for a comfortable chair and a desk or table where you can take notes, open a book or two, and keep important papers handy. Bookshelves, room for a computer (if you use one), and drawers for storing paper, pens, pencils, and other supplies are all part of a well-arranged work space. Hang a bulletin board on a wall to post items such as a calendar for marking important dates, like due dates for your assignments.

You should also have a wastebasket and an easily visible clock.

Having plenty of light is essential. Your eyes can feel strained, and you may tire more quickly if you try to read and write in a dimly lit room. You need a good desk lamp and an overhead light. And though you may think it's not important, attractive decorations, like pictures, are a good idea. Since you'll be spending a good amount of time in your work space, you'll want to make it cheerful. Also, try to choose a work space that is reasonably quiet, at least when you are working there.

Once you have your space nicely organized, make a point of keeping it orderly. It is amazing how quickly papers pile up if you let them. If you start to let it go, before long you'll find yourself staring at an enormous, messy jumble where an important assignment could vanish forever. You don't want to waste a lot of time hunting through the clutter to find some notes or an assignment. By keeping your work space organized, you will know where everything is, save time, and reduce anxiety.

Think about these points when arranging your space. While you want to be comfortable when you work, you should avoid chairs or

INSIDE SECRET

Ways to Make Space When There's No Space

Even a small work space has room for plastic or cardboard filing boxes that you can put in an out-of-the-way corner or even under the bed. Available at office supply stores, these boxes are perfect for storing papers and supplies. Remember that the smaller your available space, the more important it is to keep it neat.

couches that are so cozy you might doze off during a study session.
Consider possible distractions, like televisions, telephones, and stereos.
What you do to avoid these things depends on how you deal with distractions. If having a TV nearby may tempt you to watch videos or a
rerun of your favorite sitcom, put the set elsewhere—like in a closet. If
you cannot hear a phone ring without answering it, perhaps you should
turn off the ringer. If you can play soft, pleasant music as background
while you study, fine. But if you like your music so loud that it interferes with your thinking, then you may have to put that music system
in the basement. Remember that the function of a work space is *work*.

Ready Set...

REVIEW

Get Ready to Study

Here are a few questions to consider while arranging your work space. Only you can decide what's right or wrong for you. But if you're still confused about what to do, try talking to a parent or teacher about it.

1. Next to my work space there's a window that I like to look out of and daydream. What should I do?
   a. Arrange my space so that my back is to the window when I study.
   b. Draw the curtains to block the view from the window during study times.
   c. Teach myself to avoid daydreaming during study sessions.
   d. All of the above.

2. My little brother and his friends have noisy play sessions when I am working. What should I do?
   a. Ask them nicely to play more quietly because I have to work.
   b. Find another, quieter work space.
   c. Wear a set of earplugs.
   d. Learn how to screen out the noise mentally.

3. Which of these choices would be best for me as a work space?
   a. My room, which I love but is equipped with video games, TV, stereo, and phone.
   b. The basement, which is big and quiet, but is badly lit and has small windows.

c. The den, which has a desk and bookshelves, but which I can only use at certain hours of the day.

d. The breakfast table, which is well lit and available most of the day, but where people come through a lot and where I cannot leave things overnight.

For each of the following areas where you might have a motivation problem, come up with an incentive that would enable you to accomplish your goal. Decide whether a short-range or a long-range approach to motivation is more useful. Be sure to consider your individual habits and preferences in making your choices. Again, don't worry about right or wrong answers—the right answer is the one that works best for you.

1. I find reading and analyzing poems very boring, but I really need to get a good grade in English— and I have to read and analyze a lot of poetry this term.

2. I'm supposed to study for a math test tomorrow, but my favorite TV shows are on this evening.

3. I have to write a report for social studies, but it's not due for a week. Still, I haven't taken much time for research yet, and I haven't written a word.

4. This weekend, my best friend has invited me to spend a weekend with her family at a nearby beach—but I'm supposed to finish a science project that we'll present in class on Monday.

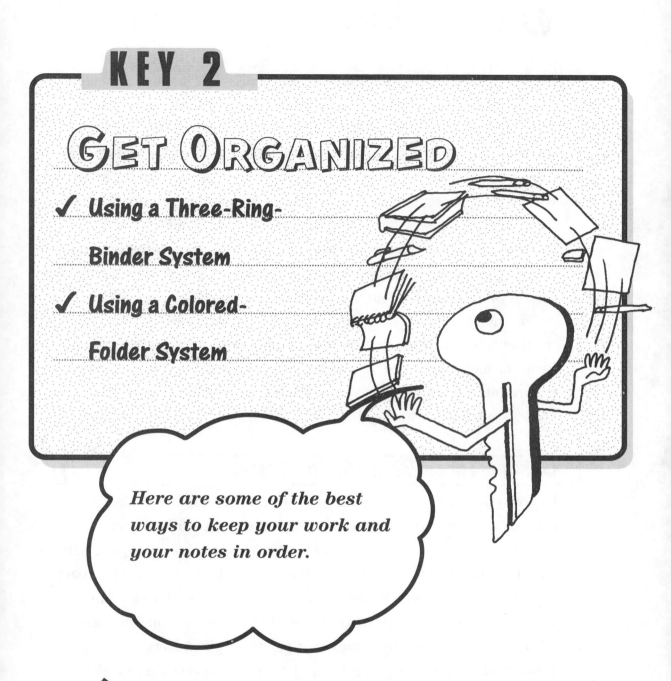

GET ORGANIZED

✓ **Using a Three-Ring-Binder System**

✓ **Using a Colored-Folder System**

Here are some of the best ways to keep your work and your notes in order.

You have your supplies, and your work space is set up. But you must take another step or two before you're ready to hit the books. Think about how you can keep your work and your notes in order. During a school term, you handle a lot of paper: study notes from class and home, handouts, assignment sheets, rough drafts, final drafts, and other items you may not even know about yet.

All this material can help you meet your goals—but it also can become a problem if you don't have a system for handling all that paperwork.

You need to keep some things handy to check from day to day. Where should they go? You may not need other papers for several weeks, but you do want to save them for when you prepare for a test, write a term paper, or compile a portfolio. Where can you put them so they're out of the way but you know how to find them later? Some items you will have no further use for and can throw out, but are you sure which ones? Do you want to risk finding out that some vital notes somehow disappeared into the wastebasket?

You don't need to feel overwhelmed by these questions. This chapter shows two possible systems for keeping everything under control. Read through it, and decide which one works best for you. You may even want to be creative and try using both, depending on what subject you're studying.

Using a Three-Ring-Binder System

One way you can organize your papers, and keep them organized, is by using a three-ring loose-leaf binder. Since you will use your binder to keep most of your valuable school notes and other papers, be careful to hang on to it. Make sure that it's sturdy: You can find flimsier binders that may cost a little less, but they may not survive an entire year. You also can use two-ring binders, but three-ring paper is easier to find in stores, and three rings hold papers in place more securely. Make sure to have a large supply of three-hole loose-leaf paper. Be sure to label your binder clearly with your name, grade level, and the name of your school and teacher.

Next, create a way of separating your binder's contents into sections for each class. One way to do this is with three-hole-punched *dividers* made of stiff, durable material. You can buy dividers in packs, and they usually come in a variety of colors. Each divider has a projecting tab, which makes it easy to turn to the section of the binder you want. Write the name of a class on *both sides*—not just one side—of the tab on each divider, and keep your notes and papers for that class in the section of the binder that follows that divider. In addition to a divider for each class, you should have a divider indicating a section

where you can store extra loose-leaf paper so you won't find yourself out of paper while you're busy taking notes.

Instead of dividers, you may prefer to use *folders* that are hole-punched for insertion in binders. Like the dividers, the folders come in several different colors. Folders have certain advantages over dividers. One advantage is that they have inside pockets, where you can put class papers that are not hole punched. Another advantage of prepunched folders is that instead of carrying your binder with you to every class, you can keep the binder in your locker and carry only the folders for the classes you are going to before your next trip to your locker. When you go back to your locker, you can put those folders back in the binder and remove the folders you need for your next classes.

If you decide to take your binder with you from class to class, carefully put any handouts, assignment sheets, or other papers for a specific class in the section of the binder meant for that class. If you misfile papers, you might forget about them or have trouble finding them when you need them.

Get in the habit of going through your binder for a few minutes every day, perhaps at the end of your study sessions. This is a good way to spot papers you have filed in the wrong section and to notice papers with binder holes that are torn. When you find torn holes, repair them right away in order to prevent important papers from being lost. Be sure that you always have a supply of hole reinforcements for that purpose.

A hole punch comes in very handy, especially if you are using a binder with sections separated by dividers (rather than folders with pockets). Whenever you get papers in class without prepunched holes, you can punch the holes yourself, either in class or as soon as you get home. Make sure you do it so the holes line up properly with the binder rings. Then insert those papers in the binder. If you keep the punch at home, be sure you have a secure place to keep the handout or other paper until you insert it in the binder.

You can get three-hole punches that punch all three holes in a sheet of paper at the same time and can be fastened directly in your binder. Or you can get the smaller, pocket-size kind that makes one hole at a time and takes up less space.

Reorganize Your Binder

Over the course of a term, as you get more and more paper, your binder can get very full. Start looking through the binder more thoroughly now and then—perhaps once a week—to look for papers you can remove in order to lighten your load. Papers you can remove fall into two categories: papers you can throw away and papers you want to keep but don't need to carry with you.

The papers you can throw away include assignment sheets for completed assignments, notes you took but now realize are no longer useful (be sure you are right in such cases!), notifications of events that are over, handouts you no longer need to consult, and material you have duplicated elsewhere.

Papers in the second category include class notes from early in the term that you may want to study later and work you may want to put in your portfolio. Store these somewhere in your home work space, where you can find them when you need them. Also, hang on to graded assignments that might be useful later in the term. They may help you prepare for a final exam or compile your portfolio. Be sure that you have a secure box or other container for storing these papers. You might get a plastic or cardboard file box with dividers and create a labeled section for each class. Arrange filed papers by class and by date.

KEY 2

LEARNING IT RIGHT

Model Binder with Labeled Dividers

This is how your three-ring binder should look. Notice that the tabs on each divider identify each class and that the class name is written on both sides of each tab. Notice also that the owner of this binder has labeled the binder with her name and the name of her school and her teacher. In addition, she has used a hole reinforcement to fix a torn hole in a sheet of loose-leaf paper. The reinforced hole and the label on the binder are *not* just matters of convenience; they are important precautions.

If you set up your binder correctly and keep the contents well organized, you can keep track of your schoolwork easily. Organization is really a matter of getting into the right habits—and using them.

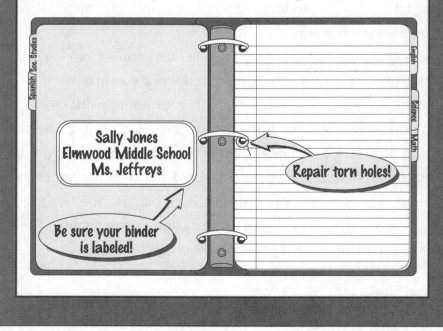

Using a Colored-Folder System

Some students find that using a big, heavy binder has some disadvantages. A binder can be awkward and hard to carry, especially when it starts to fill up with papers for every class you're taking. As an alternative, you can use separate, different-colored folders for your notes and other class papers. The colored-folder system has some advantages over the binder system. Which system you choose depends on your preference.

With the colored-folder system, you need a separate folder for each class. Each folder should clearly be a different color, to prevent confusion as to which folder is for which class. Your folders should be made of a durable material and have inside pockets in both covers. Additionally, your folders need metal fasteners that hold a supply of three-ring loose-leaf paper, the same kind that you would use in a binder. (Manila folders don't work because they don't hold papers securely. They are designed for an inside filing system rather than carrying from place to place.)

Just as you would do with a binder, see that your folders are carefully and

INSIDE SECRET

The Organization Checklist

Whether you use a binder or colored folders, draw up a checklist of the things you need each day, at home and at school, to make the system work. Make sure you have enough paper, the right folders, and any notes from home or school that you may need. Put a copy of the checklist on your home bulletin board and another inside your locker door, and look it over before you leave home and before you leave school every day.

clearly labeled. The information on the label for each class folder should include the name of the specific class plus your name, your school's name, the name of the teacher of that class, and your grade level. Write legibly, in ink that is not water soluble. To be safe, you may want to stick a *second* label with the same information *inside* the folder, in case the label on the outside of the folder becomes unreadable or damaged.

Put a supply of loose-leaf paper between the fasteners in each of your class folders. Use the left-side folder pocket to keep papers that are already graded, grade sheets, handouts, and, if you like, some scratch paper. In the right-side pocket, put ungraded assignments—the ones that you have to turn in. You might also want to keep some extra loose-leaf paper there.

You should have some hole reinforcements and a hole punch (or three-hole punch), just as if you were using a binder. As with a binder, make a habit of checking your folders to see that the pages are secure. If you spot pages with torn holes, fix the holes immediately.

In addition to your class folders, you should have one folder that you take to every class, carry home after school, and bring back to school every morning. This final folder is especially important. If you have a note from a teacher or from the school that your parents need to see or if you have a note from your parents to your teacher, carry it in that folder. You should also use it for other material that is not related to a specific class: memos on supplies you are running short of, permission slips, and—a very important item that will be discussed later in this book—your daily schedule. You might label this folder your "carrying" folder, or you can make up a name that works for you. Whatever else you carry between school and home can go in this folder, too.

As with a binder, go through class folders often. Look for papers that you can throw away and papers that you do not need to carry daily but can file in your work space.

One advantage of the colored-folder system over the three-ring-binder system is that instead of dragging a bulky binder everywhere you go, you can take only the folders you need for a specific class, plus the carrying folder, and leave the rest in your locker. In the morning, you can take only the books for your morning classes, along with the appropriate folders, out of your locker. Don't forget to check your class folders to see that they have enough loose-leaf paper. If they do not, add some from the storage folder. Leave your other folders and books in the locker. All the papers you need for class are already in each class folder from the previous night.

After class, put any papers you get into the correct pocket of the class folder. When you go to your locker, you can remove what you need for your next classes and leave the rest behind. At the end of the day, take the books and folders you will need at home that evening, and leave the rest in your locker. It may sound complicated, but you can get used to it easily.

Which system should you pick? Either one can help you keep everything organized. The only wrong choice is to have no system at all.

Three-Ring Binder	Colored Folders
All papers are in one place and easy to keep track of.	Papers are in several places.
A binder is less likely to be misplaced.	A folder is more likely to be misplaced.
A binder is heavy and awkward to carry.	Folders are light, easy to carry.
Paper may be easily inserted or removed.	Paper is difficult to insert or remove.
A binder is more expensive to replace if damaged.	Folders are less expensive to replace if damaged.
If a binder is lost or misplaced, papers from all classes are lost.	If a folder is lost or misplaced, papers from only one class are lost.

Ready Set...

REVIEW

Getting Organized

Once you decide whether to use a three-ring binder or colored folders, you may want to do some preparation.

If you plan on using a binder, write out a label for the cover, including the necessary information and making sure that your writing is easy to read. Then write the labels you plan to use with the dividers or the folders for each section of the binder. What classes are on your schedule? Might you need additional sections—for extra paper, outside classes, or extra-curricular activities? Arrange the binder to fit your needs.

If you choose to use folders, decide on a color code. Make a list of the available colors, and decide which color is appropriate for each subject and which colors you might use for extra paper and a carrying folder. Write a label for the cover of each file, including the necessary information and writing clearly.

Which of the following papers could you throw away, and which ones should you keep, at least for the time being?

1. An assignment detailing what is required for a project that is due next week

2. A test that your teacher has graded and returned

3. A permission slip to be signed by your parents for a class trip next month

4. A list of selections from your English textbook, to be read during the upcoming term

5. A handout advertising the school picnic that took place two weeks ago

6. An essay that might be included in your end-of-the-year portfolio

MAKE THE MOST OF CLASS TIME

✓ **Taking Notes**

✓ **Active Listening**

✓ **Asking Good Questions**

✓ **Participating in Class**

Discussions

Your attitude determines whether the time you spend in class every day is worthwhile and challenging. Make the most out of the time you spend in class.

ecause you spend a great deal of time in class, it makes good sense to make the most of it. You can do this in several ways, even just by sitting in the ideal place in the classroom. Also, consider the good and not so good ways to listen in class. You will find it very useful to learn about a technique called "active listening."

You can help yourself a lot by using an effective note-taking technique. Also, try to understand why it helps to participate in class. Is it a good idea to ask a lot of questions? What can you do if you are shy about speaking up in a roomful of people? This chapter gives you tips about all of those subjects—and a lot more.

Taking Notes

Preparing for class is important. Keep only your binder or folder, a pen, and your textbook (if you need it) on your desk. Put everything else out of the way. Be sure that you have plenty of loose-leaf paper and that your pen actually writes. (Keep a spare pen handy, just in case.) If time permits before class begins, quickly review what you learned in your most recent assignment. You are getting ready to take notes.

At the top of your notes, write your name, the name of the class, and the date. The date helps keep all your notes organized. Leave a wide margin, at least an inch, on one side of the page; it is useful for later additions. Write your notes in ink, since pencil fades and smears easily. Be sure to keep your notes in your folder or binder. When you take notes in class, don't try to write down every word your teacher says. (Your main purpose isn't to make a show of looking very busy so your teacher is impressed.) Keep two goals in mind: making a well-organized record of the *important* information you hear and *understanding* what it means and how it connects to other things you learn. Taking notes means being selective in what you write and thinking about what you hear.

Do not try to write too much. Good note takers write 20 percent of the time and listen the other 80 percent . You don't have to take that literally, but remember the basic point. Your aim is to write down significant ideas and facts, not the trivial details. There is no point in writing down facts you already know, like the number of months in a year.

You should also write your notes in your own words. Since you are the one who reviews your notes, make sure you use language that you understand, and write legibly. Of course, some information should be written exactly as your teacher gives it. For example, if your teacher writes down information on the chalkboard, copy it in your notes. Do the same with any definitions of unfamiliar words. If your teacher doesn't write the definitions of the words on the chalkboard, try to write down the spoken definition as accurately as possible.

Be careful to listen for *verbal cues*—hints that a teacher uses to indicate that something important is coming. These are phrases like "pay particular attention to," "the basic idea is," "don't forget that," and "most of all, remember that." Carefully write down whatever follows such cues, and make a mark in the margin, such as an arrow, to call your attention to its importance for later review. If you have time, write those marginal marks in red ink, so that you are more likely to notice them.

Your note taking can be simplified if you create a code, or *short-hand*—a system of symbols and abbreviations that help you write notes more quickly. The following chart gives examples of this kind of shorthand.

Abbreviation or Symbol	Meaning
+	and; also
<	less than
>	more than
w/	with
wh/	which
w/o	without
esp	especially
∴	therefore
*	most important
v	very
→	resulting in
≈ *or* appr	approximately
nv	never
imp	important
≠	different from
=	the same as
cen	century
gov	government

LEARNING IT RIGHT

Model Notes from a Social Studies Class

Ann Andonn

10/10/05

Social Studies

Industrial Revolution — from 18th cen. on

in red ink Factories built, _city pop., _pop. on farms.

Inventions → more indust. prod.

✱ V. imp.—more middle class in cities → diff. soc. class syst.

Some opposed machines, esp. old-time craftsmen.

Did Luddites attack other kinds of factories? Lost trade, money.

What happened to Luddites?

Luddites = Eng. group, early 19th cen., attacked textile factories, wrecked machines in reaction to loss of work for weavers who couldn't compete. Named for

? Ned Ludd, their namesake-founder, not a real person.

If a teacher uses an unfamiliar word and gives no definition, write the word down and circle it (possibly in red ink) so you can look it up later. Also, underline or mark any points that seem unclear. You can ask about them at the end of class.

Do not stop taking notes just because your teacher opens the class up for discussion and questions. Other students might say something of value. Or your teacher may make a significant point while answering a question.

Review your class notes as soon as possible after class ends so you will retain a clearer understanding of them. If you see that anything is illegible, recopy it neatly while it is fresh in your memory. For an idea of what a useful set of notes might look like, see the sample notes for a social studies class (on page 29).

Active Listening

What does "active listening" mean? Does it mean that you run in place when you're in class? No, what you want to keep active in class is not your body but your *mind*. To put it another way, you should work at keeping your focus on what your teacher—and other students—say in class.

Active listening is focused listening. When your mind is alert and you are full of energy, you are more likely to pick up what might escape the attention of a drowsy student. One way to boost your ability to stay focused is by getting enough sleep. If you stay up watching a late show on TV or chatting on the phone, your energy and concentration levels get low, especially later in the school day. You may find yourself nodding off in afternoon classes. That can also happen if you eat too much at lunch. So be sure to get your rest, and eat right at lunchtime.

Make a point of getting to class on time. When you miss the beginning of a lesson, you may miss hearing the purpose of the lesson. Avoid falling behind in your assigned reading and home study. If you fall behind, you might find yourself unable to follow a lesson that is based on what you were supposed to have read the night before.

Screening out distractions when you're in class is also important. If you have problems or worries on your mind, try to put them aside during school hours. You may find it hard at first, but you'll see that it should get easier in time. (Of course, if you have a big problem, you should discuss it with a school counselor.) Outside distractions can also cause problems. If you find that sitting near a window tempts you to daydream, take a seat farther from the windows. If possible, stay away from students who are likely to be distracting—students who whisper, giggle, pass notes, or click their ballpoint pens.

Focus on Your Teacher

When you focus on watching your teachers, you soon realize that they (like most people) use *body language* to emphasize their spoken words. Don't ignore body language. You can use it to great advantage. A teacher who wears eyeglasses might have a habit of taking them off before making an important point. Some people have a way of folding their arms across their chests or pausing and looking around a room before saying something especially significant. Perhaps your teacher may turn away from the chalkboard and look at the class as a way of signaling that really meaningful information is coming. If your teacher slows down to emphasize a point or speaks more loudly, take note of it. If you are aware of these signals that most people use to highlight their speech, you can improve your ability to get more from a class.

Pay particular attention to anything a teacher *repeats*. Repeated statements are apt to contain valuable information. Also, take special notice of the beginnings and ends of lessons. Teachers often use these times to summarize the most important point in a lesson. If you need another reason to get to class on time and concentrate up to the last moment, now you have one. Active listening, like many other worthwhile habits, gets easier with practice. Learning this skill will help you in many areas of your life for years to come.

Asking Good Questions

Asking questions is one of the most valuable ways for students to participate in class. You should not hesitate to ask questions, especially when something in a lesson puzzles you. Do not feel embarrassed about asking questions. Teachers generally appreciate questions because they show that you are taking an active interest in the class. Also, when you ask a reasonable question, other students in the class probably need the answer as much as you do, so you are helping everyone—even if the other students are too shy to say so.

This does not mean that there is no such thing as a bad question or that you should ask questions constantly. Students who raise their hands every minute and ask questions that are better off unasked are definitely not candidates for their teacher's favorite student. There are good and bad questions—and good and bad times to ask them.

Construct a Good Question

Perhaps the worst kind of question is one that you should already know the answer to because it was covered in an assignment you should have read or was explained by the teacher recently. By asking it, you let the teacher know that you are not keeping up with the work or are studying it carelessly. This is another reason for completing all of your assignments on time.

The best questions are based on what is being taught in class and what you were assigned to read. In phrasing your question, ask it in a way that connects it to the material you are learning. This sends the message that you are keeping up with the work and actively thinking about how the lessons and assignments relate to one another. In other words, it may not be terrible to ask, "Ms. Smartz, what does 'federalism' mean?" But it would be better to put it like this: "Ms. Smartz, I read that both Madison and Jefferson were Federalists. But you just said that they disagreed with each other on some issues. How could they belong to the same party yet disagree like that? Maybe I don't understand what 'federalism' means." The two questions are the same, but the second version ties it to other material.

Know How and When to Ask Questions

During a lesson, if your teacher says something that puzzles you, first make a note of it. Don't ask a question about it right away—unless you must have an immediate explanation to understand the rest of the lesson. If you can still follow what the teacher says, wait for a more appropriate time. Be sure that you have your question jotted down, and put an arrow or other notation in the margin so you know where to find it. The teacher may provide your answer either later in the lesson or in response to another student's question. If that does not happen, then wait until the teacher asks for questions or pauses to answer a question

INSIDE SECRET

Prepare a Few Questions in Advance

Prepare two or three questions for your class the night before, based on recent reading and class lessons. Write questions that predict what you may learn in the next class and that indicate whether your thoughts are related to what the teacher wants you to learn. Look over your questions before class, check off any that get answered during the lesson, and ask the unanswered ones after class or at another appropriate time.

KEY 3

from someone else. At that point, raise your hand, wait to be recognized, and then ask.

In general, the best way to pose a question is to raise your hand and wait for your teacher to acknowledge you. However, if he or she is not in a position to see your raised hand, such as when he or she is facing the chalkboard, and you need an answer to understand the lesson, you may *politely* excuse yourself for interrupting and ask to be heard. If you do it right, your teacher should have no problem with your interruption. Whenever you ask a question, do it respectfully and in a way that shows your interest in the material. Do *not* express boredom, frustration, or annoyance in your language, tone of voice or in any other way.

Participating in Class Discussions

Class participation can vary a lot from one class to another. In some cases, teachers spend most class time doing the talking, with only a short period for questions and virtually no time for an exchange of ideas among students. Other teachers—or the same ones in different situations—encourage debate and use students' questions as a springboard for active discussion of the course material by all students who want to take part. Sometimes teachers switch between those two (or other) formats. Whichever circumstances you find yourself in, participate as actively as you can. Taking part in class can help you learn more and get better grades. Because many teachers value class participation, they are apt to give higher grades to students who actively contribute to class discussions.

This does not mean that the only reason for taking an active part in class is to make a good impression on your teacher. In fact, trying to dream up questions or class contributions just to make yourself look good can be a bad idea. Acting that way can waste everyone's time.

What is the value of student discussion? For one thing, students often contribute valuable information that they get from outside reading. Or you might hear something in class that escaped your attention when you were doing the homework assignment. Also, students have different viewpoints, based on their background and experience, so they may come up with different and interesting conclusions. An exchange of ideas, points of view, and new information can make class discussion both interesting and useful, if you come to it with an open mind and pay attention.

Unfortunately, some students are shy and have difficulty speaking up in front of a room full of people they do not know well. If you happen to be one of those who suffer from this problem, try to overcome it. One way to feel more confident in yourself is to keep up with your work and go to class prepared. Also, make a point of sitting in the front of the room, especially if you always try to sit all the way in the back, where you might be ignored. It is harder to avoid participating when you're sitting up front, so just changing your seat may force you to act in a new, more outgoing way.

You can also practice out loud, in the privacy of your room. This may sound silly, and you might *feel* silly at first, but it isn't silly at all. Try standing in front of a mirror and then asking a question as if you were in class. While you watch yourself talk, you become comfortable with the sound of your own voice, and you see yourself as other students see you. Give it a try. Prepare a few questions based on a recent assignment, and try asking them aloud in front of a mirror. Then, ask the same questions in class. The technique does work.

You are sure to find that the more you get involved in class discussion, the easier and more natural you feel doing it. Speaking up can help you in important situations, such as in meetings at your workplace or while working on projects with fellow employees. Someday you may look back and wonder why you had such a problem in the first place.

K
E
Y
3

REVIEW

Class Participation

1. To practice active class participation, prepare three questions you can ask in one of your next classes. Here are some questions to get you started.

   - **What class should the questions be for?**
     Perhaps you should choose the class in which you already feel the most comfortable or where you know that the teacher welcomes questions.

   - **What have you covered in recent assignments and classes?**
     Jot down a summary of what you are currently studying in that class, and think of the questions it raises.

   - **How can you best phrase your questions?**
     Remember that you want to tie the questions to the course material. Keep the questions as clear as possible. Practice asking them at home once or twice, and check them over before you go to your class.

   Good luck!

2. Practice your note-taking technique by summing up the following passage about pasteurization. Sum up the important details, using abbreviations and symbols where needed.

   Pasteurization is a way of killing harmful organisms, such as bacteria that can cause milk and other foods to spoil and can even make those foods harmful to eat or drink. The process was named for the scientist who invented it, a Frenchman named Louis Pasteur. He found that milk and other foods in which bacteria might grow could be preserved by heating them over a low flame for a period of time. This killed the bacteria and other organisms so that the food could be kept for a longer time without spoiling and without affecting its taste. Since refrigeration had not been invented at the time, Pasteur's discovery was very important to people who produced and sold foods that were subject to spoilage. Even today, most milk is pasteurized before it is sold to the public.

MAKE THE MOST OF HOME STUDY TIME

✓ **Setting Goals**

✓ **Eliminating Distractions**

✓ **Finding the Right Reading Strategy**

✓ **Using the SQ3R System**

✓ **Using Memorizing Strategies**

✓ **Studying for Tests**

NO TV

NO VIDEO GAMES

NO PHONE CALLS

> *Working at home is as important as working in class but can be trickier. For one thing, more distractions lie in wait.*

Temptations, like TV, stereo, and video games, surround you. Who at home makes sure that you study when you should? Who sees that you've done your work correctly? If no one does that for you, you must rely on yourself to have discipline and not lose sight of what you must accomplish. Even if someone at home checks on you, eventually you will be on your own and will need to know how to motivate yourself. So it's best to learn self-discipline now.

The best way to start a project or assignment is by deciding on your goals. This is true for long-term projects, like reading and reporting on a book, and short-term ones, like meeting your daily work schedule. When you know what you need to do and have a goal in sight, you can stay focused more easily. As you read assignments and know what you need to learn, you absorb important information and retain it more effectively. This chapter explains how you can make the most of your home study time.

Setting Goals

When the time comes to work, do you just open a book and dive in? That sounds great, but you might save some time if you first decide how to complete your assignment successfully. Not every word you read is equally important. By thinking about your goals, you can focus on what is important and not get sidetracked. The time you spend mapping out your goals can help you channel your thinking in a productive direction.

Different courses require different approaches to reading. Reading assignments for a science course generally demand careful reading, during which you should pause frequently to grasp the principles and then connect them to the assignment as a whole. For a social studies text, you may need to focus on a series of events and think in larger terms about how one event leads to the next. In that case, you may read at a steady speed and wait until the end to make a list of how the events tie together.

In other words, you read in many different ways, and the best way to begin any of them is to get a sense of what your goal should be.

Begin by determining what kind of material you are about to read and for which class. You can learn your goals for the assignment by glancing over—or *skimming* through—the text. Skimming is a helpful reading technique because it gives you an overall sense of your assigned reading material. (You can learn more about it in the following discussion of "Finding the Right Reading Strategy.")

Clarify your goals for an assignment or project by writing them down. The following sample shows the kind of questions you can ask yourself to help yourself set your goals.

Eliminating Distractions

Unless you live near the South Pole, you must cope with distractions. The phone rings, your sister plays loud music, or a friend drops by to hang out. Other potential distractions are always nearby, too: the TV, video games, the local mall with its wonderful shops, the balmy spring day outside your window. Somehow, you have to keep those tempting or annoying intruders from getting in your way. It is not always easy. But it is almost always possible to control.

When it comes to appealing gadgets like televisions, stereos, and video games, the solution is in your hands. *Anything* in your work space that you cannot trust yourself to have around must go. Unplug it. Remove it. Or move yourself. Be honest with yourself in deciding whether you can resist distractions.

As for the phone, yes, most people reach for it whenever it rings, but no law says you have to. If other family members can answer it, let them. Ask them to take a message if someone calls for you. They should be happy to help you work. If nobody else is available to take calls, you can let the phone ring, especially if you have voice mail or an answering machine. If you have a cell phone, turn it off. If you *must* answer it, take a message and get off quickly, with a polite explanation

LEARNING IT RIGHT

Sample of Possible Goals for a Reading Assignment

Place a checkmark next to all items that apply to your goal.

I am reading this . . .

___to prepare for a test.

___to understand a main idea rather than specific details.

___to discuss tomorrow or at a later date.

___to learn a group of facts.

___to review materials I have already studied.

Once I finish the assignment, I should . . .

___have mastered what I read.

___understand a concept and be able to apply it to other material
   I have studied.

___understand the characters and the setting in which they live.

I should be able to remember . . .

___details and facts.

___the author's point of view and intent.

___the order in which events took place and their causes and effects.

___the relationships among characters.

___comparisons and contrasts between the people and places

   described and my own world.

___steps in a scientific or technical procedure.

that you are studying. That explanation should also be enough to turn away unexpected visitors who show up at your door.

When it comes to noisy family members, ask for your family's help. Explain that you are setting aside a regular time period for studying and that you would be grateful if they could keep the noise down, especially near your work space. You might have to bargain a bit, but you are likely to reach an agreement if family members understand that you need to study. It is certainly worth a try.

You're likely to get more cooperation from your family if you establish a regular study schedule and stick to it. If everyone knows that you're trying to work between the hours of 4:00 and 6:00 on weekdays, for example, they'll be more apt to coordinate their own schedules with yours. On the other hand, if your study time varies from one day to the next, it may not be as easy for all people in the household to adjust their lives to fit your needs.

Concentrating

When you *concentrate* on your work, all your energy and attention is focused on that work. The ability to concentrate, or focus, is a practical skill. Lack of concentration can result from several possible sources. Distractions generally come from outside sources, like ringing phones. But some concentration problems come from within you. What you may not know is that you can take action to correct and prevent those lapses in concentration.

Some concentration wreckers are physical. Lack of sleep can mean low energy and poor focus. The solution: Get enough sleep. There is no fixed rule on how much sleep is enough, but if you find yourself drowsy during the day, you need more sleep than you are getting. Sometimes you may feel drowsy when you are getting sick. The nasty symptoms of a

KEY 4

cold, flu, or other illness can lower your energy and make it hard to focus. As a rule, when you enjoy good health, your work benefits.

Poor concentration can be linked to *food*. Hunger attacks take your mind off work, a problem you can solve by eating a healthy snack during a work break. If you eat big dinners, you may have trouble concentrating afterward. You may feel sluggish because your body is working to digest all that food. Eating lighter dinners often gets rid of after-dinner drowsi-

ness. In addition to eating a suitable amount of food, make sure that the foods you eat are healthy. High-fat foods and overly sweet snacks lead to poor nutrition, which can affect your ability to concentrate.

Sometimes poor concentration has a mental, rather than a physical, cause. If you see a project as a huge, overwhelming job, you may get discouraged and find it hard to stay on track. You can deal with that by breaking the project into small, manageable steps. If you find yourself daydreaming about fun times or worrying about problems with a friend or family member, try to direct your focus back to your work. When you remain focused, you find that study time flies by without your noticing it.

Boredom is likely to leave you fidgety. When you find a subject or an assignment boring, you can lose focus. You may drift away from your work

INSIDE SECRET

Getting Others to Respect Your Space

Think of the place where you work as *your space*, where you call the shots and others must respect your wishes. If you use that right properly, you will find that your family and friends are willing to accept it and give you the respect you deserve.

KEY 4

into a pleasant daydream only to realize suddenly that a lot of time is gone, with nothing to show for it. How can you stop this? Make an effort to develop a better attitude toward homework. When you start, take a moment to focus your attention and remember your top priority. Look for ways to develop more interest in the subject, or think of motivations to keep going.

Never force yourself to work for long, unbroken periods. They tend to leave you tired and unhappy. Schedule your work time in the form of shorter periods, and allow short, regular breaks between those periods. To keep your breaks short, you might even use a timer. Give yourself a reward for your diligence. Call a friend to chat, take a walk, or have a snack.

Remember that you can improve your ability to concentrate by applying yourself. The more you work at it, the more natural it becomes.

Finding the Right Reading Strategy

What? You need a *strategy* to read? Yes, you get more from assigned reading by choosing the right reading strategy for the material. This may sound complicated, but you probably already use different techniques for different types of reading without realizing it. For instance, the way you read your science book differs from the way you read fiction.

You can choose from three basic reading techniques: *scanning*, *skimming*, and *reading for detail*. You also may combine two techniques to get the most out of your assigned material. Once you know what the different strategies are, the process of selecting the right one is easy.

Scanning

When you scan reading material, you go through it very quickly—too quickly to read all the words. When you want to search for a specific item, such as the definition of a word in the dictionary or a date in an encyclopedia entry, you scan to find it. You also may scan a reading assignment when you pick it up for the first time, to get a sense of its organization. Is it broken down into chapters? Are there pictures, charts, or graphs? Does it contain an introduction or a glossary? Scanning is a speedy way either to locate a specific fact or to get quick information about assigned material.

Skimming

Skimming, like scanning, is done quickly. But while you should scan to find out how an assignment is organized, you should skim to get a sense of the general contents of the assignment. Like scanning, skimming does not involve reading every word, but unlike scanning, skimming involves reading *some* of the words. You use this method to "pre-read" a reading assignment in order to get a sense of what you need to focus on when you read it carefully. Skim material to spot main ideas and topics and to see how chapters and sections of the material relate to one another.

When you skim, read titles and subtitles, check paragraphs for names, dates, or lists, and look at any illustrations, charts, and graphs and their captions. In addition, it is good to read the first and last paragraphs of chapters and sections and, if you have time, the opening and closing sentences of paragraphs. Be sure to read any questions after paragraphs and chapters, because they give a good sense of what the assignment is about. Before you go back for a careful reading, jot down what your pre-reading suggests you should look for when reading thoroughly.

Reading for Details

When you read an assignment for details, you *do* need to read all the words. Use this technique when you need to absorb a lot of information. While you read at a slower rate than you do when you scan or skim, your speed can vary, depending on the subject matter and the difficulty of the text. You can adjust your rate as you go, looking for the speed that allows you to retain what you need from the selection.

K
E
Y

4

When you read poetry, you are likely to move particularly slowly. Technical writing, such as a science book, also requires slow and careful reading. You can probably read other types of nonfiction, like history, at a faster rate. And you may read fiction even more quickly. But each assignment is different. Be flexible and adjust your rate to fit the specific text and your reading purpose.

Adjusting Your Reading Rate

Technique	Reading Rate	Use	Appropriate Material
Scanning	Very fast—do not read most of the words.	Search for specific items, like a word definition or a person's name; get a general sense of the structure of the assigned reading.	Dictionary or other reference book, textbook, list, index
Skimming	Fast—do not read many of the words.	Discover main ideas and topics; look for connections among chapters and subsections.	Pre-reading assigned texts, fiction, nonfiction
Reading for details	Slow enough to read all the words—rate varies depending on the type of material assigned.	Read for facts and ideas; look for connections between ideas in the text and in previous reading; take notes.	All assigned reading

When reading for details, stop often to sum up what you have read and to consider how it connects to earlier reading and course work. Depending on how long and detailed the text is, stop after each paragraph, section, or chapter to jot down summaries in your notes. Pay particular attention to text framed in a box or printed in *italic* or **boldface** type or printed in any other way that emphasizes its importance.

If you are reading a magazine or a book that you can write in, mark important passages with a highlighter or marker. If you cannot mark the text directly—if the text is in a book you do not own, for instance—copy important passages down in your notes if they are short, or sum them up in your own words if they are longer. When questions occur to you while you are reading, jot them down in your notes, too, and mark them with a highlighter or underline them, perhaps in red, so that you will be sure to take special notice of them. Do the same with unfamiliar words if you cannot figure out their definition from the context. You can then look for answers to your questions in other sources or ask in class.

When you read a book, also pay attention to what is *outside* the main text, including *prefaces*, *introductions*, and *forewords*, if any. These sources can provide useful information about the author and the author's purpose for writing the book. In the back of the book, a *glossary* defines unfamiliar words and a *bibliography*, or list of books on the subject, suggests other sources for you to look at. An *appendix* offers other useful information. Also, check the bottoms of pages for *footnotes*, which also include useful facts.

Using the right mix of the three reading techniques helps you to take in more from—and get the most out of—all your reading assignments.

Using the SQ3R System

Many learning systems aim at making students into better readers. A professor named Francis P. Robinson from Ohio State University developed an especially successful system during World War II to help teach army trainees. It is still used today at all levels of education. It is called *SQ3R*, after the initial letters of the system's five steps: **S**urvey, **Q**uestion, **R**ead, **R**ecite, and **R**eview. SQ3R works especially well with textbooks and is effective with other material, too. Some students find that it takes a little getting used to, but many

KEY 4

students who stick with it—as well as their teachers—report that it is extremely useful. This section tells you something about it so that you can give it a try and decide for yourself.

(S) Survey

When you use SQ3R, you begin by surveying your assignment. First, look over the entire selection. Read all the titles and subtitles. Next, skim the material, taking note of all text in *italic* or **boldface** type, because it signals significant themes and topics. Look at illustrations and other graphics, like charts and graphs. Try to get a broad sense of the content of the assignment, concentrating on the main ideas. End your survey by reading the final paragraph and any questions at the end of the assigned selection.

(Q) Question

Look at the topics in **boldface** or *italic* type, and use each of them to create a question that starts with one of these words: *who, what, where, when,* or *why.* Write these questions down. Next, estimate the amount of time you will need to read the selection for details. As you read, check off each question as your reading provides the answer. Keep all of your unanswered questions for further research or class discussion.

(3 Rs) Read

Read the selection for details, focusing with care as you go. Pay particular attention to important details and to examples that support the major ideas. After reading each section, go back and underline in ink or highlight the important facts. If you cannot write in the book, write down the facts instead, and keep those notes in your binder or folder.

If the selection describes a sequence of events and the order is important, be sure to write the events down in their exact order. Try to retain in your memory as much of the important information as you can. (See "Using Memorizing Strategies," beginning on page 48, for helpful tips on training and strengthening your memory.)

(3 Rs) Recite

This step is based on the fact that many people retain information better when they recite it, or say it aloud. After you read and note or highlight each section of your assignment, stop to answer your written questions as you discover the answers to them. You can give your answers silently if you prefer, but reciting them aloud is a useful memory aid. Phrase your answers in your own words. In order to preserve these answers, jot down a few words as cues. After you finish the assignment, give yourself a quick quiz on what you have just learned. Mark any points that you have trouble recalling.

(3 Rs) Review

When you find that you cannot recite the main ideas or details of certain sections of an assignment, review or reread those sections. Take time to look for ways to tie the different sections of the whole assignment together. For example, are they linked by a chain of cause and effect? Are they all examples of a common theme? After reviewing in this way, write down a summary of your reading in your own words. In doing this, you are creating a study guide for the assignment that you can visit later. Use it to review the information the next day, a second time two days later, and two times more within a week of your first reading.

The SQ3R system may help each student in different ways and to varying degrees. Results show that many students benefit from its use, so

KEY 4

give it a try. Allow yourself several weeks to get familiar with it so that you can get a good sense of whether it works for you. The following SQ3R reading chart can help you keep a record of the experiment. One sign that it works for you is that you remember more of what you read. You might also discover that you are using less time to get good results as you read.

Using Memorizing Strategies

A good memory is one of the most valuable qualities you can have as a student. Do you find yourself envying some classmate who simply glances over assignments and remembers every word? If so, bear two things in mind. First, students who think that a good memory can replace good study habits will some day discover they are wrong because eventually they will be expected to learn a large amount of information that requires lots of studying—no matter how strong their memory may be. Second, you *can* improve your ability to memorize. This section tells you how—even if you think your memory is pretty good to begin with.

Graphic Organizers

Graphic organizers are tools that help you organize information in a visual way that's easy to memorize. They help you improve your memory in two ways. First, the process of creating them helps you learn. Second, their organized format helps you remember facts and ideas when you review them later. Several types of graphic organizers are useful.

Charts

You can use several types of charts to arrange a lot of information in an orderly way. These types include: **box charts** (like the one on the next page); **Venn diagrams,** for comparing and contrasting (see

KEY 4

Recording Your SQ3R Progress

Subject: _____

Assignment:	Assignment:	Assignment:	Assignment:	Assignment:	Assignment:	Assignment:
Due Date:	Due Date:	Due Date:	Due Date:	Due Date:	Due Date:	Due Date:
Time Spent Reading:	Time Spent Reading:	Time Spent Reading:	Time Spent Reading:	Time Spent Reading:	Time Spent Reading:	Time Spent Reading:

Appendix A); **concept maps,** for showing how ideas are connected (see Appendix B); **flow charts,** for showing sequences of events (see Appendix C); and **time lines,** for noting a sequence of historical events.

Tables

A table is a compact arrangement of information in rows and columns. If you need to organize information about the nations of the world, for example, and show facts like population, capital cities, industries and products, and official languages, a table is a good form to use.

Outlines

One good way to keep notes for a long reading assignment is to make an outline. An outline is a summary of the basic ideas and themes in a piece of writing, with secondary ideas and subtopics for each main idea grouped under that main topic. Each subtopic or secondary heading can serve in turn as the heading of its own subtopics and secondary points. Usually, main headings are identified by Roman numerals (I, II, III, IV, and so on). Subtopics are indented under the main headings and identified by capital letters (A, B, C, etc.); their details or secondary points are indented still further and identified by Arabic numerals (1, 2, 3, and so on). As you outline, you organize your thoughts about what you're reading and create a handy study aid for later review.

Visualizing the Page

Sometimes, a picture can help you remember information much more effectively than the words on the page of a book can. For instance, instead of trying to remember the printed facts from a page of information about the state of Florida, such as the climate and crops, try creating a picture of Florida in your mind. Picture a bright sun shining down, an orange sitting on a plate, and some people sitting on a beach under a palm tree.

If you need to remember the year in which the Wright brothers first flew their airplane at Kitty Hawk, for instance, think of a rickety old-fashioned airplane just getting off the ground, with a big "1903" on the underside of its wing. If you visualize the name "Kitty Hawk" painted on its side, you are likely to remember that, too. Many people can remember dates, names, and other facts more clearly from seeing visual images in their minds than from trying to rely on words alone. You might want to add little sketches to your notes to help remember important events and dates. When words alone are not working for you, add a mental picture to your memory or a visual cue to your notes.

Memory Tricks

There are tricks that can help you use your memory. They are called *mnemonics* (the first *m* is silent). The previous visualizing technique is a kind of mnemonic. Usually, *mnemonic* refers to words or sentences you create to remember lists of things, places, or events. One well-known mnemonic is the word students use to remember the names of the Great Lakes: HOMES. Each letter of *homes* is the first letter of the name of a lake: **H**uron, **O**ntario, **M**ichigan, **E**rie, and **S**uperior. A similar kind of mnemonic uses the first letter of each item of a list as the first letter of a word in a sentence. For instance, to remember the stages in the life cycle of insects—**e**gg, **l**arva, **p**upa, and **a**dult—you might use this sentence: **E**very **l**ady **p**icked **a**pples.

Notice that the sentence does not have to make much sense or have anything to do with the idea you want to remember. But you may find it easier to remember the stages of the life cycle of insects by remembering *Every lady picked apples* than by repeating the names of the stages over and over. When you must remember not just words but their correct order, as in the case of the insect life cycle, a mnemonic sentence is more helpful than a single word. When order does not matter, as

K E Y 4

with the Great Lakes, a word works. Just figure out one with the appropriate letters.

Oral and Written Repetition

Repeating a word, or any other piece of information, is a reliable way of storing it in your memory. When professional actors memorize their lines for movies, TV, or plays, they often do it by repeating the words—sometimes many hundreds of them—over and over. One technique they may use to keep the repetition from getting monotonous is saying their lines in a slightly different way each time they repeat them. Actors who perform in a play many times find that they usually remember their words years later. Repetition may seem monotonous, but it doesn't have to be. Some people remember more clearly when they *look* at what they want to memorize, while other people remember better when they *hear* the material. You can experiment with both ways to see which one suits you best.

If your memory responds better when you say words and phrases out loud, then start doing that more. You can also record the information you want to memorize on a tape, so that you can listen to it repeatedly without straining your voice.

If your memory works better when you see words on a page than when you hear words spoken aloud, try rereading only short bits of material at a time instead of soaking up big chunks. Once you are sure you have stored one small piece of text in your memory, go on to the next little piece, until that one is fixed in your mind, too.

Flash Cards

Do you need to memorize the definitions of some vocabulary words? Do you have a list of facts to learn? Do it with *flash cards!* You can make them from index cards or cut construction paper into card-sized pieces. Write a vocabulary word, or a question, on one side of each card and the definition, or answer, on the other side. If you use index cards, put the questions or vocabulary words on the lined sides and the answers or definitions on the blank sides. To keep homemade cards in order, write a "Q" on the question sides and an "A" on the answer sides.

Put the cards in a pile with the questions facing up. Look at each card, and try to say the correct answer without peeking at the other side. Then, check to see if you got the right answer. If you did, put the card in a "correct answer" stack. If your answer was incorrect, return the card to the bottom of your main pile. At the end of the pile, go back through the cards where you missed the answer. Once more, pull out the cards that you answer correctly. Keep going through the cards until you get them all right.

Later that day or the next, repeat the entire process. You should find that before long you do not miss a single one. Keep the cards for review at a later date. If you use the flash cards for learning new vocabulary words, you might want to collect a set of flash cards for all the words you learn in the term and go through them regularly to be sure the words stay in your memory.

Working with a Partner

You may want to bring in a partner to help when you do some memory exercises. Your partner could be a classmate, friend, or family member. Sometimes memorization can get dull, so having a partner may make the process more enjoyable. Be careful, however, that it doesn't get *too*

K
E
Y
4

enjoyable. If you find that you and your partner are distracting each other, you might decide that you need to work with a different person or that you are better off working alone.

If your partner is a classmate, each of you can prepare for your session by making up a quiz based on the material you are studying. Use your quizzes to test each other's knowledge. When you do not answer your partner's questions correctly, make a note of what you missed. After you take a break, quiz each other again, and see if you now get the right answers to the questions you missed earlier.

You also can use flash cards with a partner, with one of you asking the other the questions on the cards. Just as you would do when working with flash cards by yourself, return cards to the bottom of the pile when the person being tested gets a wrong answer, and then go through the pile again and again, until the person being tested correctly answers every question. Take a short break, and then the person who had asked the questions can take a turn answering them.

Studying for Tests

How does studying for tests differ from studying for classes? For surprise, or pop quizzes, the only way to prepare is to make sure that you are always up-to-date with your reading assignments and lessons. But all other exams, including final tests for a term, require advance preparation. When you're facing an upcoming test, you'll feel glad that you kept all your notes and class papers organized and ready to review.

Tests usually involve a specific area of knowledge. Even when the test you're studying for is a final exam for a term, much of the test may focus on *facts*, rather than broad ideas. Even tests in subjects that might include essay questions, such as science, history, or English, expect you to remember specific events, reading selections, or other details from the course. Become as familiar as possible with factual details, such as the order in which events took place, the names of places and people, and the correct spellings and definitions of special words used in the content areas (such as *photosynthesis*, *immigration*, or *tragedy*).

The memorizing strategies described in the previous section are helpful when you study for tests. Mnemonics, graphic organizers, and flash cards are useful ways of arranging a lot of information in your mind so that it's ready to be recalled and written down. Studying together with partners can be an effective way to prepare for a test—assuming that you don't distract each other from the work that has to be done.

Whether studying alone or with a partner, start by jotting down the areas that you think are likely to be included on the test, and then concentrate on those areas. If you have kept up with your assignments, kept orderly notes, and studied a little bit each day leading up to the test, you can enjoy a good night's sleep and approach the test with confidence.

K
E
Y

4

Ready Set... REVIEW

Studying at Home

1. You can use several different types of charts as graphic organizers, depending on the kind of material you are working with. They include *box charts*, *Venn diagrams*, *time lines*, and *concept maps*. Look at the following ideas, and decide which kind of graphic organizer you would make to remember the information:

   a. The sequence of the major battles of the Revolutionary War

   b. A study of the differences and similarities between cold-blooded and warm-blooded animals

   c. Early European explorers of the North American continent, their areas of exploration, and their encounters with native peoples

2. Try to make up a few mnemonics for yourself. Make up a sentence that helps you remember the first six presidents of the United States: **W**ashington, **A**dams, **J**efferson, **M**adison, **M**onroe, and **A**dams. Remember that your sentence doesn't have to make sense or have anything to do with American history. What word or sentence might you use to remember the planets of our solar system? Remember—if you want to remember them in a particular sequence, such as from the sun outward, you need to create a sentence.

MAKE THE MOST OF HOMEWORK

✓ **Understanding the Assignment**

✓ **Managing Your Time**

✓ **Presenting Your Homework**

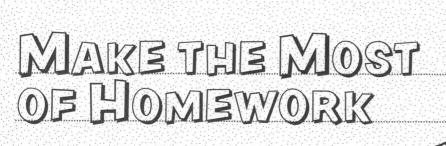

Most kids don't go around saying that homework is fun. But it actually can be fun at times—and extremely useful.

Homework is useful when you do math problems, for instance: You become better at working with numbers and get a clearer grasp of how they work. If you approach that social studies assignment in the right spirit, you can get a better understanding of people all over the world and through the ages. You can see how events from hundreds of years ago affect your world today. Try to think of homework not as a time-consuming task to get out of the way before you can have fun but as an important part of your education. And an education isn't just about getting good grades. Your education helps you understand the world around you and gives you valuable skills that you'll use now and for the rest of your life.

Doing homework is an important step toward learning to become an adult and shaping your future. The way to take full advantage of homework is to know what you have to accomplish and plan a way to do it efficiently. That can make homework an enjoyable, rewarding experience.

Understanding the Assignment

Before you start a task, know what you are supposed to do. That sounds simple, but sometimes it isn't. If you start working without understanding the assignment, your results can be frustrating, time-consuming, and—even worse—incorrect. Always try to get started with a clear idea of what you are expected to learn, and when you need to be finished.

As soon as you get homework assignments, *write them down;* do not trust them to your memory. The best way to handle this task is by using an *assignment sheet* that you take to classes with you and fill out every day. This sheet should be a form, with space for your name at the top, along with the date and day of the week. Divide the form into sections for each of your classes, where you can write your assignments and any necessary details. Include the math problems you must do, textbook pages you must read, any composition, report, or story you are expected to write—along with how long it should be—and, finally, the date when each assignment is due. Include space to jot down any errands and appointments for that day.

If you are not sure of exactly what an assignment involves, ask your teacher. That way, you are not likely to spend time writing a story about your cat's personality when your teacher wanted a report about the significance of cats in different cultures and times. Being sure about your assignments means that you won't discover that all your

Sample Assignment Sheet

Name Ellen Lyons　　　　Day Tuesday　　　　Date Oct. 19

Homework due today:

　English—read story in anthology, pp. 78–90

　Math—do Chapter 6, Problems 1–12

　Social Studies—read textbook, Chapters 9–10

Classes:

9:00 A.M.: English—read poems in anthology, pp. 34–36

10:00 A.M.: Social Studies—read textbook, Chapter 11

11:00 A.M.: Math—do Chapter 6, Problems 13–25

Noon: Lunch with Deb and Louise

1:00 P.M.: Earth Science—do research on desert environments and plants

2:00 P.M.: History—read textbook, Chapter 9, pp. 95–107

Errands, meetings, appointments:

Library (for books about the desert),

　3:15—hockey practice

　Call Grandma to wish her happy birthday

Things to remember: Read pp. 41–80 for book report due Nov. 18;

　class field trip next Wednesday—get permission slip signed!

work on Chapter 5 will not help you the next day because the class is working on Chapter 6. If a new assignment is not due the next day, be sure you know when it is due. If an assignment calls for special materials, such as art supplies or a library book, underline or circle that information so that you remember to get the materials you need in order to do the work. When you know what your assignments are, you can more easily focus on getting everything done.

Managing Your Time

How much can you get done in a day? You might be surprised
at the answer, once you start making good use of your time.
Chances are you can do more than you think. Also, when you plan your
time, you are far less likely to forget assignments or discover that the
time you needed for finishing your math problems was somehow filled
by an English assignment that isn't due until next week. One valuable
tool for managing your time is called a *to-do list*.

To-Do Lists

As you might guess, a to-do list is a list of what you need to get done in
a specific time period, like a day. Get into the habit of making a to-do
list for every day you have work to do. A daily assignment sheet like
the one just described can serve as your to-do list. If you do not use a
form, be sure to write down all your assignments in a list that you can
take home with you every day. The to-do list should include all homework assignments plus any other activities, such as meetings, practices,
or appointments scheduled for that day. In addition, write down newly
received assignments that are not due until a later date. When you get
to your home work space, jot them down on a scheduling calendar.
(Learn more about the calendar under "Scheduling.") Once you have a
complete to-do list, you can move on to the next important step in
planning your time: prioritizing.

Prioritizing

Imagine that your to-do list shows that three class assignments must be
ready the next day and two others are due next week. What should you
work on first? To answer this, you need to set up an order for your assignments. That step is called *prioritizing*. You are arranging your
tasks so that you decide which ones are urgent and which ones can

KEY 5

wait for later. In order to prioritize your assignments, you should have a list of all of them. Your to-do list is fine for this purpose. If you do not have one by now (why not?), make a list of your assignments. Mark those to be done by tomorrow with an x. Those are the high-priority tasks that you need to tackle first. But which of those should you start with?

Plan to begin with your most challenging assignment for the next day, because your energy is at its highest and because it feels good to get it done. You can then go on to the next hardest assignment, and so on, until you finish up your homework with the least demanding of your tasks. (The simplest tasks tend to be the ones that you may even find yourself enjoying—and that makes them feel like a reward for finishing the harder tasks first.) Place a number next to each assignment, making the most difficult job number 1 and giving the easiest job the last number. Now that you've prioritized your daily assignment list, you can go on to the next step in managing your time: making up a work schedule.

INSIDE SECRET

Study the Hardest Thing First

People generally want to put off the hard jobs for as long as they can. But when you take on the toughest assignment first, you generally feel a great sense of relief when it's done. That rush of relief gives you more energy to finish the rest of your work—and makes it more enjoyable because you're no longer dreading something.

Scheduling

What does it mean to *schedule* your work for a day? It means to decide roughly how much time you need for each assignment and, with that information, to work out when to begin and end each task. Begin by estimating how long each assignment should take. Deciding how much time you need is a process that gets easier as a term goes on, since you learn to base your estimates on how long similar assignments have taken. But even at the beginning of a term, you should have some sense of the time you need, based on your work pattern from previous terms and school years. Don't worry if your estimates are not accurate or if you do not schedule every minute of your allotted study time. In fact, you should try to allow room for adjustments and unexpected interruptions.

The next thing to decide is when you plan to work. Think about whether you work best in the afternoon or in the evening, before or after meals, and so on. Try to schedule study times for when you find it easiest to concentrate, although you also have to allow time for other activities you have planned for the day.

The chart on page 66 models a student's daily schedule, including her prioritized assignments for that particular day. The student with this schedule—Jane Monroe—might prepare part of the schedule the night before and fill in the rest after getting homework assignments for the following day. She chooses to read her science book early because she finds that takes more concentration than most of her other assignments. She saves her biology assignment for last because that is the subject that interests her the most, and she finds it the easiest. Notice that she gives herself breaks during her study sessions. Also, she has a book report due at a later date. Since she is ahead of her schedule for that project, she allows herself the choice of continuing to read the book or not, depending on whether she feels tired after she finishes all of her other work. Note that she is smart enough to save the fun part of her day until after she has finished all of her work.

When you set up your schedule, save the fun part of your day for last so that you can look forward to it—and really relax and enjoy it—after you have completed everything you had to get done that day.

KEY 5

LEARNING IT RIGHT

Model Study Schedule

Jane Monroe   Wednesday, Feb. 21, 2005

7:00 A.M.:	Get up; get ready for school
7:30 A.M.:	Breakfast
8:00 A.M.:	Check backpack for books, folders, completed math and social studies homework, signed permission slip for class trip, new homework assignment sheet
8:05 A.M.:	Leave for school
8:30 A.M.:	Begin classes
11:30 A.M.:	Finish morning classes; meet Gina and Marlene for lunch
12:30 P.M.:	Begin afternoon classes
3:00 P.M.:	Finish classes. Take books, folders needed for homework. Swimming practice
4:30–	Homework: math, 4:30-5:00; study science textbook,
5:45 P.M.:	Chapter 28, 5:00-5:45
5:45 P.M.:	Fifteen-minute break. (Call Marlene?)
6:00 P.M.:	Check math problems; review social studies notes
6:15 P.M.:	Dinner
7–7:45 P.M.:	Study biology, Chapter 18
7:45 P.M.:	Fifteen-minute break (e-mail Cousin Terry?)
8:00 P.M.:	Read Chapter 8 of book report book (if I'm not too tired—I'm ahead of schedule!)
8:30 P.M.:	Take it easy! TV; listen to new CD?
10:00 P.M.:	Get stuff ready for school tomorrow, wash up, bedtime!

In addition to a daily schedule, you should have schedules for long-term projects, those with due dates as much as a few weeks ahead or longer. For that purpose, keep a wall calendar—one with space for notes on each date—in your work space. You can write down when long-term projects are due and keep track of other important dates, such as final exams and class trips. When you keep a schedule marked on your calendar, you are less likely to forget about long-term assignments. After all, those due dates seem so far in the future, when you don't have something around to remind you how quickly time flies!

The best approach for long-term projects is to create a schedule for them that lets you spread the work out over the full period, until the due date. For example, consider a book report that is due six weeks after you get the assignment. To schedule the job, ask yourself these questions:

- How long is the book?

- How many pages (approximately) can I expect to read in an hour (so that I can understand the material and take notes)?

- How long might it take me to write the report?

If you believe that you can write it during a single week—perhaps using weekend time and some weekday—you can divide the reading over the first five weeks and leave the writing for the final week. Be sure you schedule enough time to write the draft and then revise and edit it.

If the book is 200 pages long, you need to read 40 pages a week for five weeks to finish it. If you find that you can read fast enough to get through 50 pages a week, you might adjust your schedule so that you don't need to read during a week when you have to study for several exams. Or you might decide to start reading right away, knowing that you have some time available in case anything unexpected comes along that might take more of your time than you had planned for. The schedule you write into your daily calendar might look like the following model.

K
E
Y

5

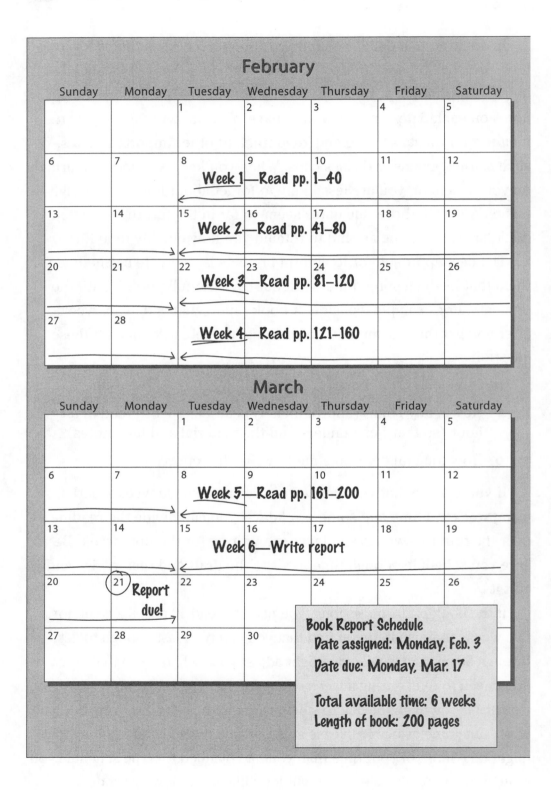

February

Sunday	Monday	Tuesday	Wednesday	Thursday	Friday	Saturday
		1	2	3	4	5
6	7	8	9	10	11	12
		Week 1—Read pp. 1–40				
13	14	15	16	17	18	19
		Week 2—Read pp. 41–80				
20	21	22	23	24	25	26
		Week 3—Read pp. 81–120				
27	28	Week 4—Read pp. 121–160				

March

Sunday	Monday	Tuesday	Wednesday	Thursday	Friday	Saturday
		1	2	3	4	5
6	7	8	9	10	11	12
		Week 5—Read pp. 161–200				
13	14	15	16	17	18	19
		Week 6—Write report				
20	21 Report due!	22	23	24	25	26
27	28	29	30			

Book Report Schedule
Date assigned: Monday, Feb. 3
Date due: Monday, Mar. 17

Total available time: 6 weeks
Length of book: 200 pages

Allowing an extra week for unexpected schedule adjustments is a smart precaution. When setting up a schedule for a day, a week, or a term, always try to give yourself room to make adjustments. In that way, if unanticipated problems come up or work moves at a slower pace than you'd hoped, you can deal with the situation.

Presenting Your Homework

Even when you hand in good assignments every day—with every math problem solved correctly, reports well written, and perfect spelling on every assignment—your grades can suffer if your work looks sloppy or disorganized. Neatness *does* count—and there really is no excuse for turning in papers that look like they fell in mud puddles or got trampled by elephants. As a rule, neatness is a matter of concentration and taking the time to do the job right.

When you write a report or essay, be sure to use complete grammatical sentences. If you write with a pen, write slowly to make your handwriting legible. Look assignments over, and if one is hard to read, decide whether it's worth recopying. If your penmanship needs improvement, consider practicing to make it better. Readable handwriting is worth the effort. It's great when you don't have to strain to figure out what you wrote in your social studies notes a month ago.

If you use a computer to write assignments, choose a simple font (type style). Avoid fancy ones with frills or squiggles. Also, remember to proofread your work—don't let the neat appearance fool you into thinking all the sentences are complete and all the words are spelled perfectly.

When you finish an assignment, tuck it away in a folder so that it doesn't get rained on, snowed on, or stepped on. It would be a shame to work hard on your homework only to have your grade suffer because it looks bad!

KEY 5

Ready Set...

REVIEW

Making the Most of Homework

1. How good are you at prioritizing a list of daily activities? Below is Jeff's to-do list for a day. Jeff likes reading poems and writing about them, which is his English assignment for the day. He does not enjoy history and has trouble remembering all those dates. Next to each activity from Jeff's list is a space for you to write a number. Imagine you are Jeff. How would you prioritize the following list of activities? Number them from 1 to 7, with the highest priority activity as number 1.

____ Call Joe about going to the mall tomorrow
____ Read two poems and writing a brief response to them for English—due tomorrow
____ Work on an earth science project on the Ice Age—due in four weeks
____ Do ten math problems—due tomorrow
____ Study chapter in history textbook—to be discussed in class tomorrow
____ Reading 30 pages of book for book report—due in six weeks
____ Watch favorite TV show, on at 5:30 P.M.

2. Create a week-to-week schedule for doing a report on a 250-page book that is due in seven weeks. Assume that the book presents no serious difficulties to read. Decide whether you want to provide time for unexpected problems that might arise. Write the schedule down in the form of a chart.

PUT YOUR COMPUTER TO GOOD USE

✓ **Organizing Your Files**

✓ **Typing and Printing Your Assignments**

✓ **Brainstorming Ideas and Making Charts**

✓ **Rewriting Your Notes**

✓ **Creating Spelling and Vocabulary Lists**

✓ **Keeping a Reading Journal**

No doubt about it, computers are wonderful tools.

You can use computers for research, for writing, for storing information, for amusement—the list is long and seems to grow almost daily. In this chapter, you can learn about ways in which you can use computers to generate better school work. You may already be familiar with some of this information, depending on whether you are already working with a computer. If you haven't had the chance to explore a computer, try to become more aware of what these remarkable machines can do.

Also, make yourself aware of a few of the computer's limitations. While a computer can improve the quality of your studying and your work, it cannot do the work for you. And if you use a computer carelessly, you can create big problems for yourself. You can lose notes or compositions *permanently* if you do not take some precautions. Computers are valuable tools—but they are not magic wands. So pay attention to the warnings that follow, as well as to the positive suggestions.

Organizing Your Files

Imagine a "system" where you take all your notes, assignments, and other papers that you collect in a school term and store them by dumping them in a box. Can you picture trying to find one item in that mess? Computer storage works—or *does not* work—in the same way. It is easy to arrange your documents and records so that you can find them again, but you need to organize everything consistently. That means making the proper use of **folders** and **files.**

If you share a computer, create a "school" folder on the monitor's desktop—the screen you see after you turn the computer on and it does its start-up routine. Give the folder an appropriate name. Depending on the computer's operating system, you might be able to use names of up to 250 characters (a character can be a letter, number, or space), and you can make up almost any name you want. (Older systems cannot use names with more than eight characters, so you may need to use abbreviations. For instance, instead of naming a folder "NancySchool," you might call it "NanSchl.") Within that "school" folder, you can make subfolders for each course. (If you do not share

LEARNING IT RIGHT

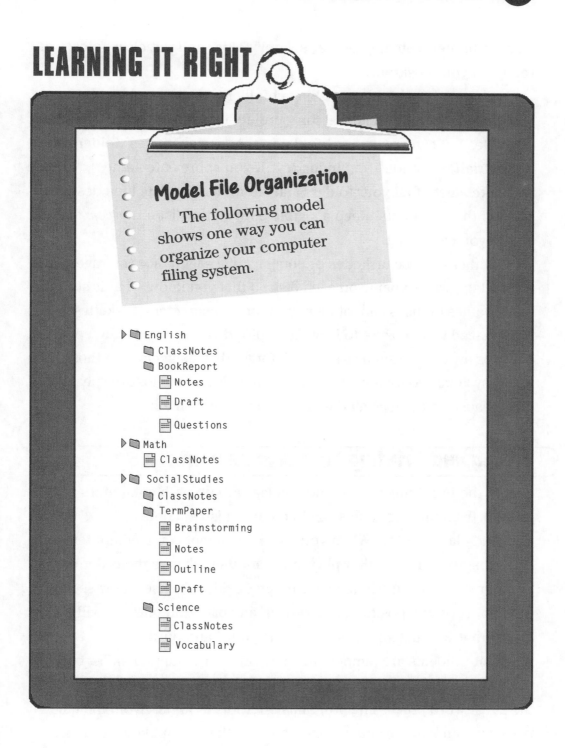

Model File Organization

The following model shows one way you can organize your computer filing system.

▷ 📁 English
   📁 ClassNotes
   📁 BookReport
     📄 Notes
     📄 Draft
     📄 Questions
▷ 📁 Math
   📄 ClassNotes
▷ 📁 SocialStudies
   📁 ClassNotes
   📁 TermPaper
     📄 Brainstorming
     📄 Notes
     📄 Outline
     📄 Draft
   📁 Science
     📄 ClassNotes
     📄 Vocabulary

KEY 6

your computer, you may skip a "school" folder and put class folders directly on your desktop.)

You can add subfolders within subfolders when necessary. If you have notes and other material for a project in a social studies class, for example, you can create a subfolder in the "social studies" folder called "IndustrialRevolution" (or "IndusRev" if you abbreviate names).

Make a list of all your folders and subfolders, and include descriptions of their contents. Keep a legible copy of this list *on paper*, filed where you can find it.

Whether you use diskettes or compact disks with more storage space for backup, write a name on each disk so that you know what is stored on it. Names of disks cannot be more than 11 characters. Diskettes can be damaged by exposure to heat, cold, dirt, dust, or magnets. Keep your backups away from such risks. Don't forget that speakers, like those in music systems, contain magnets, so putting disks too close to speakers might cause you to lose all the information they contain.

Typing and Printing Your Assignments

One of the first things most students learn to do with computers —apart from playing games—is to create finished copies of assigned class writing. When you write documents on a computer, you can substitute one word or phrase for another, change the order of paragraphs (or even whole pages if you decide to), insert new sections in a report or composition, and tidy up any bad grammar or spelling— all without wasting supplies or making your hand hurt!

Some students are tempted to show off their computer skills, but tricks can interfere with the goal of turning in good work. For instance, the latest word processing programs offer lots of *fonts*. Avoid the fancy ones, and stick to the simple kind, the ones that resemble the printing you see in most books. Two of the most popular fonts are *Times New*

Roman and *Arial*. They are popular because they look neat and are easy to read. If you feel like experimenting for fun, go ahead. But remember that frilly, cute type styles are hard to read and distracting. Save fancy type faces and clip art (the little illustrations that you can add to computer documents) for personal letters and writing.

Spell-checking programs are handy for checking for misspelled words after you finish an assignment. But remember to proofread

your writing, too. Do not depend on a spell checker to catch your spelling, punctuation, or grammatical errors.

Here is one more *very important* warning that can save you a lot of trouble: When working on documents, *always back them up!* You can set your computer to back up your work automatically at regular intervals, such as every twenty minutes. Once you set this (and you can learn how through the "Help" feature on your word-processing program), the computer does the backup without your having to do anything more until you close the document. In addition, as soon as you stop work on any file, back it up by copying it to a diskette. That way, if you accidentally delete your work or something terrible happens to your computer, you will still have a copy of your work.

INSIDE SECRET

Spell-Checking Programs Can Make Mistakes!

Spell-checking programs catch spelling errors—*unless* a "misspelled" word is a correct spelling of another word, like *there* for *their* or *too* for *to.* If you mean to type *their* and you type *there* or you mean to type *too* and you type *to* instead, the spell checker thinks that all is well. Always proofread your writing in addition to using the spell checker.

Brainstorming Ideas and Making Charts

Here are two learning techniques. Brainstorming helps you come up with ideas when you cannot seem to get started on a project. Making charts is something you might do on the computer.

Brainstorming

To brainstorm, start with a blank sheet of scratch paper, think about your topic, and jot down whatever comes to mind. Before long, the things you write down—no matter how silly or unimportant they may seem at first—suggest other ideas that then lead to still other ideas. If you keep writing down whatever comes to mind, after a while you will have a long list of ideas jotted down. Review your jottings, cross off the ones that lead nowhere, and then add any new thoughts that come to you. Eventually, you will find that you have enough ideas to get going on your composition or report. If brainstorming is new to you, give it a try. The results can be amazing.

If you work with a computer, brainstorming can be even easier. Open a new document that can serve as electronic scratch paper. Remember to give it—and *all* your documents—a name that will help you locate it when you want to return to it. For example, you might name this file "brainstorming." (For tips on keeping documents in order, refer to "Organizing Your Files"; see page 72.)

As you brainstorm, type or key in everything that comes to mind. When you review what is on your screen, copy the ideas that seem worth keeping into a *new* document, giving this new idea file an appropriate name. You can then switch back and forth between the two files, adding to the idea file until you think you have enough to get started. Eventually, you can cut and paste the contents of your idea file into a more sensible order if you decide to and then rewrite the specific ideas so that they make better sense.

Do not delete the "brainstorming" file, however. You might want to review the products of your brainstorming session again before you finish. Save it along with your idea file and any other documents for this assignment in a folder you create specially for the project. Be sure that your project folder and all the files it contains have names. Above

K E Y 6

all, *be sure to back everything up.* If you back up your files on diskettes, you may want to use a separate diskette for documents related to this assignment. If you use your current disk, which has a much greater storage capacity, create a folder for this project, just as you do on your hard drive. Brainstorming and computers are two useful study tools that work wonderfully together.

Charts for Organizing Ideas

Among the computer's many useful qualities is that it can be used to make charts that help you keep information and ideas in an orderly form. The most popular word processing programs all make it easy for you to create charts and tables that you can save as documents and fill in as you gather information. You can create a box chart or table, for example, with as many vertical columns and horizontal rows as you like. You also can create charts with the use of a *database* program, which is covered in the upcoming section, "Creating Spelling and Vocabulary Lists" on page 81.

If you are not sure how to make a chart, you can get step-by-step instructions by consulting the program's "Help" feature. The chart on the opposite page is a sample of what a student might do while finding and organizing information about the planets of our solar system. As the student collects information, she can add it to her chart. If she finds mistakes in her research, she can make corrections easily.

Charts like this one are extremely helpful when you are collecting material for projects that involve a lot of statistics that must be neatly arranged. In addition, charts can also keep track of other types of information. For example, you might want to use a chart to keep track of the facts you get when researching ideas from your brainstorming sessions. You can add or delete material as you continue your work.

As with all your other documents, give charts useful file names—and be sure to back up the files whenever you make changes in them.

The Planets

Name of Planet	Distance from Sun	Diameter	Number of Moons	Time It Takes to Go Around Sun	Temperature Range	Other Notes
Mercury	Between 28,600,000 mi (46,000,000 km) and 43,400,000 mi (69,800,000 km)	3,031 mi (4,878 km)	None	88 days	-280°F to 800°F (-170°C to 430°C)	Rotates every 58 days.
Venus	About 67,000,000 mi (108,200,000 km)	7,521 mi (12,104 km)	None	225 days	860°F (450°C)	Very bright in sky (evening star).
Earth	93,000,000 mi (150,000,000 km)	7,926 mi (12,756 km)	1	365.25 days	-129°F to 136°F (-90°C to 58°C)	
Mars	Between 128,600,000 mi (208,600,000 km) and 154,00,000 mi (249,200,000 km)	4,223 mi (6,796 km)	2	About 1 Earth year + 10.5 months	-230°F to +60°F (-140° to +20°C)	Is there, was there, life?
Jupiter						
Saturn						
Uranus						
Neptune						
Pluto	Between 2,749,600,000 mi (4,425,100,000 km) and 4,582,700,000 mi (5,900,100,000 km)	1,430 mi (2,300 km)	1	248 Earth years (!)	About -387°F (-283°C)	Can't be seen without telescope.

K E Y 6

Rewriting Your Notes

What do you do with all the notes you take during a school term—the ones you take in class, the ones you make while studying at home, the ones you make when working through overnight assignments, and the ones for researching long-term projects? One way to deal with them is to get a file drawer or box and keep all them together there, in separate folders for each class. When you have access to a computer, the solution to the problem of storing and keeping notes becomes much simpler. You can transfer them to files and store them electronically! They are easy to read, they cannot get wet or smeared or fade, and—if you take precautions—they will last through a whole term or longer.

It is true that rewriting notes, on paper or on a computer, does take time. But think of it as time well spent. For one thing, as you rewrite notes, you also review and refresh your memory of them. Since you ought to review your notes now and then anyway, the time you spend putting them in electronic files is time you would use for review. Also, as you rewrite, you can take the opportunity to reorganize your notes. You can combine class notes with home study notes on the same topic and include information that you may not have had when you took the notes in the first place. This is a good way to keep your folders or binder from becoming too full of paper. As you turn your notes into more organized and legible files, you can get rid of a lot of paper permanently.

When you rewrite your notes using your computer, be sure to include some important information, such as the names of textbooks or other sources of information, along with the number of the chapter in which you found the material and the date when you originally wrote the notes. Create a folder for each of your classes, and keep the note files in those folders. And don't forget: *Back up your files*. Otherwise, your time and work could be wasted.

Creating Spelling and Vocabulary Lists

One of the more useful types of computer programs is a *database*. While you can work with a word processing program on lists of words, facts, or statistics, database software gives you more flexibility—as long as you are not writing text. Database files are especially handy when you want to create and work with lists of words, either for spelling drills or vocabulary practice. Every time you get a spelling list, you can either create a new database file for just those words or add them to an existing file. When you take a test on those words note the ones you misspell. Later, when you can call up the file on your database, mark the misspelled words in a separate column to the right of the list of words. To work on only the words that give you trouble, create a new file that contains only the words that you have misspelled on past tests.

You also can keep a file that combines all of your spelling lists over an entire term. Database programs allow you to arrange combined lists alphabetically, using just a few keystrokes. With this master list, you can create an alphabetical list of the words you misspelled more than once and drill yourself on them from time to time. As you master the words, delete them from the list. You'll feel a sense of accomplishment as you watch the list of troublesome words get smaller and smaller.

In addition to spelling lists, you can create files of vocabulary words. When you come across unfamiliar words in your reading, jot them down. Later, find their definitions, and add the words and their definitions to your vocabulary file. You can then review the list once in a while to see which words you remember. Mark those that give you trouble, and delete the words that you now know. You don't have to

K
E
Y

6

insert new words alphabetically, since the program automatically re-arranges the list that way whenever you make changes.

Be sure to give your spelling and vocabulary files appropriate names, and as always, *back them up*.

Keeping a Reading Journal

Whenever you read a book, whether for a class assignment or for personal enjoyment, make notes about the book, and add them to a journal, or record, of all your reading. You can do this on index cards and keep them in a file, perhaps arranged alphabetically by author. But a database file is another handy way to keep your journal organized and current.

A reading journal can serve several purposes. If you want to choose a book to write a report on, or if you want to find a good source when preparing for a test or if you want an assignment, or if you want to recommend a good book to a friend, you can quickly find it on file.

In your journal entry for each book, include the date you finished the book, the title and author's name, the type of book (fiction, nonfiction, humor, history, and so on), and the age level for which it is appropriate. Add the copyright date, the subject matter, a summary of the contents, and your reaction to the book. When you want to call up a particular journal entry, you can do that by using the title or author's name. Remember to back up your journal whenever you add a new entry.

Ready Set.. REVIEW

Putting Your Computer to Good Use

1. The following example shows what a reading journal entry might look like. Try it yourself. Choose any book you've read recently and fill in your own journal entry.

Date book was finished: _____

Title: _____

Author: _____ Copyright date: _____

Type of book: _____ Age level: _____

Subject: _____

Summary: _____

_____

_____

_____

_____

My opinion: _____

_____

2. Try organizing a folder and file system that you might use for your current school term. Create and name folders for each course, and create subfolders and files as needed. As part of the review exercise, make a list of the folders, including their names and descriptions of their contents.

KEY 6

GO THE EXTRA MILE

✓ **Fine-Tuning Your Skills**

✓ **Setting Up Study Groups**

✓ **Working for Extra Credit**

✓ **Making the Most of Teacher Conferences**

If you believe that the other chapters of this book have helped you to improve, then the following tips and suggestions can help you aim a little higher, stretch a little farther, and accomplish even more.

A re you someone who enjoys a challenge? Do you have a hunch that you could do even better in school but haven't discovered just how much you can really accomplish? For students who want to test their limits and get even more out of the time and energy they put into schoolwork, this chapter can help. Follow these suggestions to sharpen your skills and learn ways to pick up extra credit and tackle more demanding goals. If you're not quite sure whether you're ready for this, keep reading. You might feel inspired to raise your expectations. After all, you *are* capable of more than you think—when you put your mind to it!

Fine-Tuning Your Skills

Not sure what "fine-tuning" means? A mechanic making delicate adjustments under the hood of a powerful sports car is fine-tuning the engine to improve its performance. An athlete who spends time at the gym to develop certain muscles is fine-tuning his or her body to get more out of workouts. Fine-tuning helps you gain an extra edge. You can fine-tune your study skills to improve your performance in school even more.

Listening

Of all the skills discussed in this chapter, listening seems to be the easiest to do. You've already learned how to become an active listener: Make sure your energy level is high, have the right attitude in class, and concentrate so that you notice not only what your teacher says but his or her body language and other cues as well. One way to keep your focus sharp is by preparing an index card to bring to class with you. On one side of the card, jot down a few points that you expect the teacher to discuss, based on recent lessons and homework assignments. On the other side, write down the following headings, with room for a few sentences under each: "Surprises"—points the teacher brings up that you didn't expect; "Errors"—points that you'd misunderstood in recent studying, together with corrections; and "What's Coming"—a few predictions of what might be coming in future lessons and reading assignments. During the course of the class, check off those points you thought would be covered on the front of the card, and write down any "surprises" and "errors" under the appropriate headings on the back of the card. After class, but before you do your homework for that class, jot down a few predictions under "What's Coming." Filling in this information is likely to help you stay focused and strengthen your comprehension of the subject.

Speaking

There's no better way to sharpen your ability to speak than by speaking. One of the best tools to help you with this is a little audiocassette recorder. If speaking in public is a problem for you, spend some time talking into a recorder. Start by reading from a book, a magazine article, some poetry—read something that you like, and record it. Afterward, play it back and listen to yourself. If you haven't done this before, it is likely to sound strange at first, but you will quickly get used to the sound of your voice.

Once the strangeness wears off, you can think about how you sound as you listen yourself read. Do you, as a listener, have trouble understanding what you, as a speaker, are saying? Do you mumble? Do you speak too softly to make yourself clearly understood in a classroom? These are problems that you can fix with practice. By focusing on your articulation, you can learn to say words more clearly. The same thing is true of speaking louder. After a while, you can record yourself asking questions or explaining reading assignments in your new, improved speaking voice.

In addition, as you become used to the sound of your voice, you'll feel more comfortable listening to it. As you become more comfortable, you are apt to lose your self-consciousness. And self-consciousness may well be the primary reason for a habit of mumbling or speaking very softly. The more confidence you have in your ability to speak out, the more active a classroom participant you are likely to be.

KEY 7

Reading

Your reading can provide you with more than information. While you read, look for ways in which authors make their points, describe characters and settings, and use their craft to communicate to readers like you. In your reading journal, you can even jot down technical tips about how a specific writer achieves effects with words. Pay attention to the ways in which an author uses language to make a setting vivid, or even quote passages that you find striking.

If you start paying close attention to the mechanics of writing as demonstrated by writers who appeal to you, you're not only learning from the substance of your reading assignments but you are also learning from their style. This can be especially true of poetry and prose assignments for English class. Notice how authors use figures of speech, for instance—metaphors and similes—to liven up their work. This helps your reading comprehension and can help make you a better writer, too.

Writing

It is true: A great way to improve your writing is by reading observantly. As you develop a greater awareness of the style employed by writers you admire, you can look for ways to use some of the same devices in your own work.

Make a point of reviewing your writing, but not immediately after you stop working. Let some time pass, perhaps an hour or, if convenient, a whole day. That way, you are more apt to review your work as if you were a reader looking at someone else's work. Ask these sorts of questions:

- Does the material succeed in persuading me, the reader, of the soundness of the arguments?

- Are there sequences where the logic is weak?

- Are there places where I might have used a more effective means of expression?

- Are there poorly chosen words I can replace or phrases that now seem unclear?

- As I think back to the work of other writers I know, is there something they use that I could try?

When you are satisfied with your writing, always be sure to proofread, and make any necessary corrections before handing in your work. Misspellings, incorrect grammar, and unclear punctuation make a bad impression when you write for others. Take pride in your work, and make sure it looks neat.

Thinking

Just as physical exercises help keep your body fit, *mental* exercises can help build your brain power and improve the way you think. Chapter 6 describes one of the most useful mental exercises: *brainstorming.* Brainstorming can rouse your mind to come up with original ideas, make connections between far-ranging facts or ideas that might not otherwise occur to you, and stimulate a free flow of thought.

Analysis is a useful technique for learning to see two sides of an issue. Rather than simply accepting some concept or idea and filing it away in the back of your mind, examine it. Ask yourself why a certain statement is true. If it is true, ask yourself, "How does it apply to other things I study—or does it apply at all?" Try to use analysis regularly, especially when you are reading other people's opinions, such as in newspaper editorials.

Also, try to develop mental *flexibility.* Minds, like bodies, can become stiff and rigid, qualities that can get in the way of clear thinking. Being open to new ideas and unusual approaches to questions is important because it allows you to find fresh, new approaches to answering questions and solving problems. Mental stiffness, for instance, caused many people in the world to insist that the earth was flat, even when evidence began to show that this could not be so. Always be ready to consider new points of view and to weigh all sides of an argument before reaching a decision.

Setting Up Study Groups

Study groups are a great way for small numbers of students to work together. These groups can range in size from two or three students to six or more, but they shouldn't get much bigger. When a dozen students try to work together regularly, they're likely to have scheduling problems and get distracted more easily.

Students in study groups meet regularly to discuss class work and help one another with assignments and lessons. A good way for these groups to function is to choose one group member to set an agenda for each meeting, based on the class's current lessons and assignments. It is up to the group to decide whether the same person should take on this responsibility regularly or rotate the job among all of the study group members.

Study groups have clear benefits. Members of small groups are apt to share the same attitude and motivation toward their studies so they are

INSIDE SECRET

Important Skills

You can improve your efforts in these important skills by fine-tuning the following qualities:

Listening: curiosity, energy, willpower

Speaking: self-confidence, relaxation, reflection

Reading: questioning, reviewing, awareness of style, awareness of purpose

Writing: self-evaluation, thoroughness, appreciation of reading

Thinking: flexibility, openness, analysis

able to focus without being distracted by someone who may not be interested. Also, one group member may grasp certain class material more thoroughly than the others and so can help those who need assistance. Those who need assistance in one area may, in turn, be more knowledgeable about other points and return the favor.

When you set up a study group, you must arrange a few things at the beginning. Members of a new study group should get together after school to work out the details. They need to decide *when* and *how often* to meet. Meetings work best when they take place on the same days and times each week, though adjustments can be made. Next, the group should decide *where* to meet. Meetings can rotate among the homes of the members, but if one member has a perfect place to work and volunteers it, that can be even better. All group members should share the responsibility of providing snacks or refreshments, if there are going to be any, and the responsibility for cleaning up after sessions. At that first meeting, everyone should write down his or her address and phone number on a contact list. A group member with a computer can make copies of the list so that every member has the information.

If the group has trouble staying focused because a particular member or members cause distractions the group's makeup may need to change. When they are properly organized, study groups can help the performance of all the students involved.

Working for Extra Credit

Students take on extra-credit projects for different reasons. Teachers frequently give students the chance to do special projects for extra credit so that they can improve their final grades for a course. Extra-credit projects also offer students the opportunity to extend their knowledge of a subject by applying their class learning to areas that the class as a whole does not cover. In such cases, students can get a deeper, more detailed understanding of the subject.

While many extra-credit projects are done as written papers, extra credit can be earned in a number of ways. Students often do science or art projects, develop computer programs, or create portfolios. In some cases, students design their own extra-credit projects based on a strong aptitude in a subject they are taking or on an outside interest they want to pursue. These students come up with ideas for independent projects, then develop them, and finally take them to a teacher for approval.

If you choose to work on an extra-credit project, be aware that you are likely to be working on your own. Although you can check with your teacher now and then if questions arise, do not expect your teacher to be your private tutor. He or she has many other responsibilities, so expect extra credit to be based on *your* extra work. Before making a decision to work for extra credit, carefully consider what it involves.

Accepting the Challenge

Before doing extra-credit work, be aware that simply deciding to tackle an extra-credit project doesn't mean anything in itself. What matters is *completing* the work successfully. This is true whether your goal is to improve your final grade or learn more about a subject that you find

KEY 7

interesting. Nobody gets a reward for deciding to enter a long-distance race and then dropping out near the starting line.

Take some time and care in making a decision about extra-credit work. For an idea, take a moment to review "Learning It Right" on page 95. Remember, this has to be done in addition to your regular class work, extracurricular activities you take part in, and the rest of your regular routine, including spending time with friends, sleeping, and eating. First, you should decide whether you are willing to take time away from other pursuits, like things you do for fun, since the rest of your activities—like classes, studying, sleeping, and eating—are indispensable.

Second, you must decide whether what you get out of completing extra-credit work is worth the effort. If your goal is to improve your grade for a class, perhaps your time might be better spent studying harder or paying more attention in class.

On the other hand, if you take on the challenge of extra-credit work, you are likely to find that working hard for a successful result is very rewarding. You may find that with your new and deeper understanding of your chosen field, you have discovered an even greater interest in the subject, one that might lead to more serious study of this area. When your work comes to a successful conclusion, you can feel more confident in both your learning aptitude and your ability to work independently. The teacher for whom you do a successful project may develop greater respect for your skill and persistence. If after weighing the pluses and minuses carefully, you decide to go ahead, then see what extra-credit projects your teacher has in mind. Or think about coming up with a project of your own.

Suggesting Your Own Projects

If you decide to suggest your own idea for a project, begin by explaining to your teacher that you want to do an independent project. Ask the teacher to approve the topic and, eventually, to evaluate the finished

LEARNING IT RIGHT

Model of a Proposal for an Extra-Credit Project

Date: 10/10/05   Date Due: 12/5/05   Total time for project: Ten weeks

Subject: Young Theodore Roosevelt—Theodore Roosevelt's boyhood years

Research Material (to date)

Books

Jean Fritz, Bully for You, Teddy Roosevelt! New York: G. P. Putnam's Sons, 1991.

Herman Hagedorn, Boy's Life of Theodore Roosevelt. New York: Harper & Row, 1950.

Lois Markham, Theodore Roosevelt. Broomall, Pa.: Chelsea House, 1987.

Allan Ness, Young Theodore. 1978.

Steve Potts, Theodore Roosevelt, a Photo-Illustrated Biography. Mankato, Minn.: Bridgestone Books, 1996.

Shelley Swanson Sateren, ed., Boyhood Diary of Teddy Roosevelt. Mankato, Minn.: Capstone Press, 2000.

Magazines

Daniel Lynch. "Roughing It with Teddy." Western Magazine.

Sarah Paulsen, "The Boy Who Became Theodore Roosevelt." History Magazine.

Interviews:

Martha Stanley, Associate Professor of History, Hofstra College

Stephen Pierce, Adjunct Professor of History, Long Island University

This report will describe the boyhood of Theodore Roosevelt, how he overcame childhood illnesses, his adventures as a young man, and how they affected his later life.

work. Once you find that your teacher is willing, you need to choose a specific idea. It may come from a school course, a book, a newspaper article or television show, a hobby, or an interesting fact you learned from a conversation with a friend or family member. Jot down a list of possible ideas for a project; you can add to the list by brainstorming. Narrow your list down to a few likely possibilities.

Consider the amount of time you can devote to the project. If an idea seems too broad, look for a way to narrow it so that you can do all the necessary work in the available time. If you have more than one possible choice, pick the one you like the most. If research is required, look for research material. (Another book in Wiley's Keys to Success series, *How to Write a Great Research Paper*, explains ways of doing research successfully.) Go to the school or public library and check for books and periodicals. If necessary, ask the librarian for help in using the computer system that lists the library's resources, and learn how to locate relevant articles from magazines. Look at the books to see if their bibliographies name additional sources you could use. If you think of people who might be helpful, find out if they are willing to be interviewed.

Once you have enough research material to begin, consider the time you have, and create a schedule. Divide the available time into blocks for doing the research, including any interviews or field trips you might plan, writing an outline of how the project will work, and actually preparing the project. Be sure that your extra-credit work does not get in the way of your regular course work. Also, keep in mind that even though your teacher has expressed a willingness to help, this is *your* independent project, and the major responsibility for staying on schedule and doing the work is yours.

Making the Most of Teacher Conferences

You may decide to have a conference with a teacher to plan an independent project, sort out a problem that you are having with the class work, or clarify an assignment that puzzles you. That conference is sure to go well if you do a little planning ahead of time.

When you need to see a teacher one-on-one, figure out in advance what you want the conference to bring about. Go over how you plan to ask for the conference; write down your thoughts and review them before seeing the teacher. Look for a chance to talk to the teacher when he or she is not too busy with students or staff to focus attention on you. The best time is likely to be just after your class ends. If a conference is not possible at that moment, be flexible about arranging it at a later time. If necessary, make an appointment for the end of the school day.

Open the conference constructively by saying something positive, about the teacher or the class and what you hope to accomplish. Keep your words, tone, and manner polite and respectful at all times. Never give a sign of impatience, anger, or disrespect. Be prepared to take notes on what the teacher says. Make a point of expressing your gratitude for the teacher's time and advice, and be prepared to follow up with the advice you're given. If appropriate, suggest that you meet with the teacher again after some time has passed, for an evaluation of how your work in the class has progressed during the interval.

If the teacher suggests how you might get more out of the class, take those suggestions with an open mind, because they are probably worth your attention. It is important to remember that your teacher is not making suggestions simply to find fault. He or she is offering advice in order to help you succeed in class and is pleased to have you ask for help.

KEY 7

Ready Set...

REVIEW

Going the Extra Mile

1. Answer the following questions to see where you should improve your approach to studying. Circle questions to which you answer no. Be honest in your evaluation.

Do I want to study more and learn more? _____

Do I have a well-organized work space? _____

Do I make a daily work schedule? _____

Do I stick to my schedule and not get distracted? _____

Do I have a system for keeping all my notes and other papers in order? _____

Do I keep good class notes? _____

In class, am I an active listener? _____

Do I participate in class discussions and ask questions? _____

Do I have a system for studying textbooks? _____

Do I use SQ3R for my reading assignments? _____

With long-term projects, do I make a schedule and stick to it? _____

Do I get my work done before moving on to fun things? _____

Do I get enough sleep? _____

Do I make sure I eat a healthy diet? _____

(Continued)

2. Based on your self-evaluation and your school record, how might you go about fine-tuning your study skills? How can you make more efficient use of your study time, improve your attitude, or produce better results given the time and energy that you devote to school? Consider your answers to these questions, and write down the areas that you see as your strengths and those that leave room for improvement. For each area in which you could do better, jot down a few suggestions on how you might achieve the desired results.

KEY 7

Appendix A

Model Venn Diagram

A *Venn diagram* is a type of chart that is used for comparing and contrasting two subjects. The example below shows similarities and differences between mammals and reptiles. The diagram has two overlapping circles, one for each subject. The similarities are written in the overlapping area. The qualities belonging to only one group are written in the unshared part of the appropriate circle.

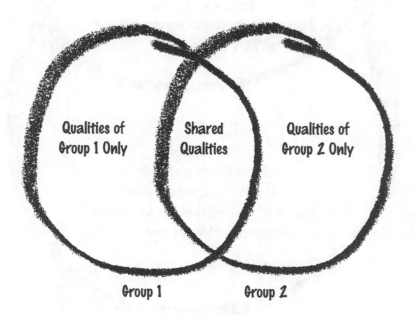

Mammals
- Warm-blooded
- Covered with hair
- Bear live young
- Live on all continents
- Carnivores and herbivores

Shared
- Have backbones
- Breathe with lungs
- Have complex muscular nervous systems
- Vary greatly in size

Reptiles
- Cold-blooded
- Covered with scaly skin
- Most lay water-tight eggs
- Live on all continents except Antarctica
- Are carnivores, herbivores, and omnivores

APPENDIX B

Model Concept Map

A concept map is useful for brainstorming sessions or for showing how a main idea leads to secondary ideas. They, in turn, can raise other ideas. In this example, lines between ideas demonstrate how one concept is linked to the next.

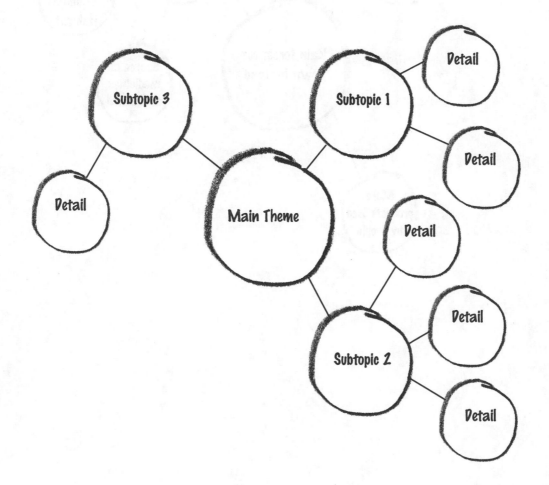

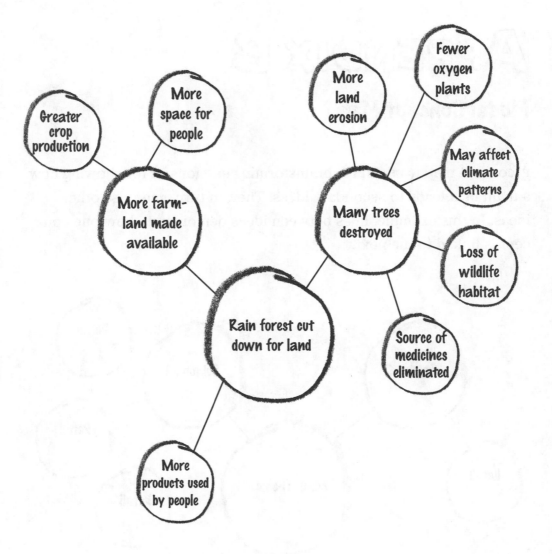

APPENDIX C

Model Flow Chart

Use a flow chart to show how subjects connect to each other in a sequence. The example below shows the life cycle that is typical of most insects.

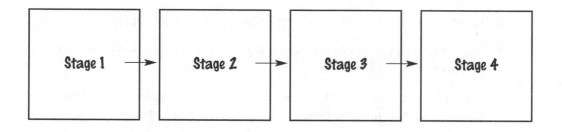

Life Cycle of Insects

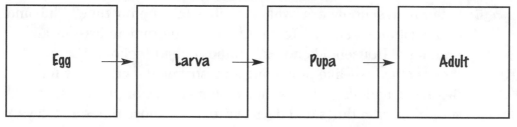

APPENDIX D

Self-Quiz for Schedule Planning

When you set up a work schedule for a day, week, or term, begin by asking yourself certain questions. Your answers to the following questions can help you plan your schedule. Note that some of the answers are apt to change over time, while others will remain the same.

1. At what time(s) of the day do I work most effectively? In the afternoon? Before dinner? After dinner? During the evening?

2. How long can I keep working effectively without taking a break?

3. How much time should I allow myself for breaks between work sessions?

4. Which of my courses do I find the easiest or most enjoyable? Which are the most challenging or the dullest? Here is a list of my classes, in order from the least to the most demanding. (It's best to tackle assignments for the most difficult classes *first* and save the easiest work for *last*.)

5. Other than schoolwork, what activities take up my time? Club and organization meetings? Team practices? Instrument lessons and practices? Household chores? Studies outside school? (Some of these activities—like practicing an instrument—can allow for flexible scheduling. Others, like club meetings or practices, are set for specific times and days; write down those times and days.)

6. What *long-range* projects, such as book reports, term papers, or extra-credit work do I need to keep in mind in setting up my schedule?

7. If I plan to study with a study group, take the schedules of the other group members into account. What are their schedules for meeting at certain days and times?

Index